Praise for *The Beekeeper*

"Why is it that some organizations thrive while so many others struggle? Why is it that some in an organization buzz with incredible energy, radiate passion, and are ready to change the world, while others disengage and count down the minutes until Friday afternoon? Whether you're working to build human capital or shift organizational culture in a sustainable way, *The Beekeeper* will inspire your leadership team to challenge the status quo while taking care of those in your hive."

—Thomas C. Murray
Director of Innovation, Future Ready Schools®
Best-selling author of Learning Transformed *and*
Personal & Authentic

"Written in the parable style of authors like Patrick Lencioni, *The Beekeeper* provides readers with a new way to look at the role as a leader. Catherine, the main character and CEO of a fledgling company, visits a highly functioning farm, which only works because of the healthy beehive at the center of the farm. By understanding the different ways all members of the beehive function, she is able to renew and restore her leadership and her company. One of the most innovative parts of this book is the narration at the end of the book by a bee that is "on the wall" back at the office. This bee provides a narration about how key workers at the company interpret Catherine's words and use them to transform themselves and their role in the company. The book is highly readable and provides any CEO with new ways to look at their job and how to communicate with others to be the best they can be."

—Dr. Bryon Grigsby
President and professor of English
Moravian University

"A rich and well-crafted story that metaphorically—and literally—reveals to us what bees have known all along about effective leadership. Every leader and would-be leader will benefit from the lessons learned from the Beekeeper!"

—Dr. David M. Kopp
Vice provost, Extended Learning & Graduate Studies
Barry University

"*The Beekeeper* is a powerful reminder that each of us is engaged in a perpetual state of be(e)coming. The gifts of this beautiful story are the possibilities for personal and professional growth evident in each moment. An invitation to embrace what happens when we allow moments of serendipity to seep in; when we create space and allow others to be nourished and nurtured alongside us. The beekeeper's parable and its lessons are powerful, profound, and pragmatic. Here we find great treasure in ourselves and all the special creatures in our world – the winged and the two-legged alike."

—Laura Kellers Queen, EdD
Founder and CEO
29Bison

"I started reading *The Beekeeper* from the prospective of finding balance in my personal and professional life. As the pages turn quickly, so does the mind, to the ability to use the life lessons on display here, to apply practically to any team or organization that is looking to improve culture, performance, and ultimately defining 'success' on their own terms.

The Beekeeper is a tremendous life lesson on balance, finding your passion, and building a team and culture. The answers are not in complicated Ivy league textbooks; in contrast, they exist everywhere on H. Ives Family Farms."

—Anthony J. DaRe
CEO, BSI Corporate Benefits LLC

"If you care about organizational culture, this is a must read! I picked up this book and realized 109 pages later that I hadn't moved. It's a compelling story told through a leadership lens that's persuasive and inspiring. I eagerly await the next book by Desiderio & Frino.

—Dr. Nicole Loyd
Executive vice president for University Life
COO, Moravian University

"This enticing introspection of a woman optimizing and transforming her business's culture while juggling the daily complexities of family life provides powerful life lessons manifested by the simplicity of changing one's daily perspective, their lens."

—Lib Obeid
Author, motivational speaker
senior consultant, Financial Services and Risk Management
Ernst & Young

"Energizing and soul-nourishing and elevated my thinking toward greater purpose and professional goals."

—Steph Vaughan
Owner, SOLDIERFIT

"Amazing read. I can't wait to start recommending this book."

—Ony Momah
Physician assistant, orthopedic surgery OAA
Founder and CEO #SWEATMindset

"A great read and lessons learned. A wonderful reminder that transformation begins where we least expect it, which is outside of the workplace. Live life with your eyes wide open and you will find your beehive. The message is simple: Go pollinate the world."

—Dan Carusi
Cofounder and CEO
Red Paint Consulting

"*The Beekeeper* is a modern, yet timeless tale of nature revealing powerful organizational lessons we all can apply to become more effective in our personal and professional lives. This quick and powerful story will be one you revisit again and again as you become the beekeeper of your own business and watch it thrive through applying these simple and practical principles."

—April O'Leary
President, O'Leary Publishing

"*The Beekeeper* will inspire all who read its transformational tale to lead with a Be mindset, become the very best version of themselves, and Be extraordinary for the people they serve. This leadership guide transcends titles and industries and galvanizes the leader in all of us to remain true to our purpose, follow our passions, pollinate our world, and nurture the Beekeepers that surround us every day."

—Drew Hinkel
Director, human resources
East Penn School District

"*The Beekeeper* is a must read for anyone looking for a refreshing leadership pick-me-up or an academic text providing valuable insights. It's a quick read with an easy-to-relate-to fable format. It's not just a feel-good story, it provides specific illustrations to the reader with a practical paradigm for how to BE a more-effective leader of a team. Katie and Mike have produced a functional bestseller."

—Dr. Larry Ross
Professor Emeritus
Florida Southern University

"As a leader, I recognize it is important to self-reflect and make sure I'm being the source for positivity and growth. This book reminded me I need to focus on that, while being vulnerable at the same time. It also made me realize my strengths as well. I'm good at giving credit where credit is due and recognizing my team for their achievements. I strive to be the Be Keeper of my family and team! I loved the book and think it would be helpful to many entrepreneurs!"

—Kristie Tapper
Certified sports nutrition consultant, personal trainer

"As an educational leader who thrives on uplifting and building capacity in those around me, I am elated to have the opportunity to use this wonderful fable to empower both my school community and own family. As we emerge from the global pandemic, to get results, schools must shift mindsets, embrace organizational change, and BE transformational. *The Beekeeper* is a heartfelt story that is sure to inspire you to BE the best version of yourself in whatever seat from which you lead. This book will help you to choose a lens of how to BE, enabling everything around you to flourish as a Be keeper."

—Tara
Elementary principal in East Penn, SD

THE
Beekeeper

A LEADERSHIP FABLE

THE

Beekeeper

POLLINATING YOUR ORGANIZATION FOR TRANSFORMATIVE GROWTH

Katie P. Desiderio *and* Michael G. Frino

WILEY

Library of Congress Cataloging-in-Publication Data

Names: Desiderio, Katie P., author. | Frino, Michael G., author.
Title: The beekeeper : pollinating your organization for transformative
  growth / Katie P. Desiderio and Michael G. Frino.
Description: Hoboken, New Jersey : John Wiley & Sons, Inc., [2023]
Identifiers: LCCN 2022054076 (print) | LCCN 2022054077 (ebook) | ISBN
  9781394165261 (hardback) | ISBN 9781394165964 (adobe pdf) | ISBN
  9781394165278 (epub)
Subjects: LCSH: Leadership. | Corporate culture. | Organizational
  effectiveness. | Organizational change.
Classification: LCC HD57.7 .D49345 2023 (print) | LCC HD57.7 (ebook) |
  DDC 658.4/092—dc23/eng/20221116
LC record available at https://lccn.loc.gov/2022054076
LC ebook record available at https://lccn.loc.gov/2022054077

COVER ART & DESIGN: PAUL MCCARTHY

SKY10049077_061323

The Beekeeper *was born on the back of a pizza box on May 2, at 8:01 p.m. in a suburb of Chicago. Katie and Michael met in graduate school while obtaining their doctorate in Organizational Learning and Leadership and have been research partners since 2011. Little did they know that 18 days later, it was* **UN World Bee Day,** *which was established in 2018 to protect and preserve our great pollinators who provide growth for all of us!*

Contents

Contents

CHAPTER
1

Before

They say that big events happen in threes. For Henry Ives, this could not be truer. As he sat at the kitchen table of his childhood home, in suburban Chicago, he was reflecting on his parents' warmth, grit, and character. These traits had been instilled in him throughout his life.

Life event number one had occurred only six months earlier. The family had known that Henry's mom was in poor health. His children had lovingly called her Grandma, and she had been a good one. Henry and his wife, Catherine, had prepared their children, Levi (8) and Helen (6), for Grandma's passing. Catherine's sister and her husband had also prepared Beau, who was only 5 years old. They all had the opportunity to grow up with Grandma and were grateful for that.

They had not been prepared when Beau's parents left this wonderful world when they were in a motor vehicle accident. Henry and Catherine had promised that they would be Beau's guardians should anything happen, and now Beau was part of their family.

Now Mom had passed away. Henry had just finished cleaning out his family house for the new owners. They wanted to keep the kitchen table and chairs, and that was the only thing left in the house. Spread across the kitchen table were family pictures, letters, and assorted documents Henry had found in a box. One last box, one last piece of family history in the home he had grown up in.

He stared at the larger 8.5 × 11 sealed manila envelope on the table. Unbeknownst to Henry, opening this envelope would change the course of his life.

As Henry slit open the flap on the envelope, his curiosity was piqued. He pulled out a folded, handwritten note on a piece of paper, yellowed with age. It was from his father, who had passed away 20 years ago. It was dated May 20, 1964. Henry was only 12 years old then.

Henry,

I hope this note finds you as I imagine; a wonderful human being that is kind and nurturing. A while back I bought a piece of land in Iowa. It was an investment I could not resist. It was too beautiful to pass up. Here is the deed to the property, which I put in your name. The seeds here are for you. You can plant them wherever you want, but these seeds will help make the environment around you a resource that encourages purpose and happiness for others.

—Love Dad

The envelope contained a deed, a map, and a bunch of seeds wrapped in plastic wrap and masking tape, with black marker descriptions printed across the tape. He read the names on the masking tape: sunflowers, clover, black-eyed Susans, lavender, mint, elderberry, snapdragons, zinnias, and dandelions. The deed indicated that the property was about 2,000 acres, roughly 3 square miles, purchased May 20, 1954, for $5,600.

He smiled and chuckled, thinking this was more stuff to deal with, but that reminded him of all the loss, and he held back tears. He knew his father had wonderful intentions.

He opened up the map and looked for the property. It was in the middle of nowhere in Iowa, but not far from a main highway and with a stream running through a large lake. He put the seeds back in the envelope, folded up the map, and set the envelope aside. *This was life event two!*

As he drove away from Chicago, Henry looked in the rearview mirror at his childhood home, watching it become a distant dot. He needed to get back home to Minnesota, as he had just sold his marketing firm and was finalizing the deal. He promised to stay on as CEO to help with the transition for the next few years. His company was thriving, and the people who worked for his firm were the reason the company was able to grow so fast.

When Henry returned home, he shared with his wife the news of their recently acquired property. His wife seemed excited and equally curious. She smiled and said, "Maybe we could move there someday and raise our kids on a farm." Henry chuckled, but his mind was turning, and a lightbulb went off – the idea was not terrible. What would he do after he transitioned the company? He needed something new to keep his mind busy.

A few weeks later, Henry told his wife he was going to check out that property in Iowa. It was going to be about a seven-hour drive. Along the drive, he was possibility-focused – he was curious and intrapreneurial.

When he arrived, he parked his bright red pickup and pulled out the map of the property. The aerial view showed that the property was shaped like a teardrop. Markings indicated that the land was a combination of brush, dirt, and native trees. He got out and looked around. He could not tell where the property began or ended, but there was a path that led into the property and it looked like his truck could handle it, so he hopped back up in the cab and put it in drive.

On the property was a large lake, spanning 10 acres, and several tributaries that fed the lake; it was so beautiful.

The streams were not stagnant, nor was the lake. Henry could hear moving water, which meant there was a larger body of water somewhere upstream fueling this zenful sound.

Henry drove about 1.5 miles straight to the center of the farm. He got out of the pickup and began walking around. He found some larger stones and marked out a circle 3 feet in diameter. This spot would one day be the heart of growth. He wanted the property to be colorful, so he reached into his pocket and pulled out the plastic-wrapped seeds.

Henry walked out of the circle that he had created with the rocks and began planting his father's seeds on the property with a handheld gardening spade. He planted the sunflowers first, then he planted the black-eyed Susans. Henry made an area specifically for the clover, lavender, mint, and elderberry, just up from the circle. The snapdragons, zinnias, and dandelions were planted sporadically around the property. He listened for the water, walked toward the sound, and found another stream. He followed the stream toward the lake, planting impatiens along the way. In the lake, there were some lily pads, milkweed, and cattail. He wondered if he should have brought his fishing pole, as the lake was active. Small minnows were feeding by the bank and trying to avoid the larger fish that were jumping and rolling on the surface.

In about three years, Henry thought, he would begin transitioning this property into what would later be known as the H. Ives Family Farms. By then, Levi, Helen, and Beau would be old enough to help him and Catherine build the farm into the vision that was forming in his mind.

As Henry drove his truck back toward the main road with his windows down and the breeze hitting his face, it struck him that the red machine stood out like a sore thumb on the property. He slowed down and put the truck in park, getting out one last time to admire the property. As he turned back, Henry noticed a bee on the hood of the truck. A single bee. He smiled and got back in the truck, capturing the image as clearly as if he had taken a photograph. This spot, Henry decided, is where he would build a house, where he would return with his family. *This was life event number three!*

CHAPTER 2

Be Fulfilled

The bee...gathers its materials from the flowers of
the garden and of the field and transforms and
digests it by a power of its own.

—Adapted from Leonardo da Vinci

"Hello, this is Catherine," I answered the phone. Air pods
in and luggage in tow, I was rushing through the chaos of
the airport.

The call was from a business broker inquiring about
franchising my essential oil business. I respectfully told the
broker we were not interested at this time but was grateful
for the inquiry.

Orlando was the third city I had traveled to that month.
My first stop was Denver, where I helped a management
team of 40 sales and marketing managers. I was looking
forward to helping them build better relationships within
their teams and begin a cultural transformation to attract
and retain top talent. The recent mass attrition occurring
across many companies had placed a renewed focus on
how managers and leaders are a catalyst to a strong
organizational culture. A common theme emerged across
many organizations of trying to find out how to build
strong teams while not losing sight of organizational
traditions that have been a historic driver of growth.

It was then off to New Jersey, where an executive
leadership team of a Fortune 500 company was struggling
to break down silos where fixed mindsets were encouraging
overuse of traditions. The goal was to learn how to
effectively demonstrate agility in considering how they
could be cultural transformation stewards and impact
collective growth from the top down.

This work continued to cascade. I was so energized to
help organizations think through how they could transform

their culture. My days were filled with conversations about human beings and how to nurture growth within organizations. So many companies are trying to figure out how they can create an environment for people to bring their best selves to work and foster a sense of belonging.

As I sat in the Orlando airport, waiting to see if my flight was going to be canceled – which had been the theme for many airlines of late due to pilot shortages – I reflected on the week. I had just presented a case study on deep-level diversity at a major conference for organizational development. I'd had the pleasure of getting qualitative feedback on the work I had been doing from other organizational development leaders and practitioners. The unwavering commitment and curiosity that was demonstrated during the case study roundtable to analyze the case and provide feedback was quite telling. I was not the only one who was seeing that organizations wanted to shift their mindset about people while transforming their culture. That sentiment was all around.

I opened my calendar to look at the month ahead. It seemed that the next couple of weeks were going to be quite intense on my travel schedule. Fortunately, my DiSC™* personality style is an Si-style, which means that I am easygoing and warm, always ready to offer support, collaborate, and be a team player. I am fueled by connection, harmony, and teaching people how to build relationships while optimizing performance – together.

That's typical of someone with the Si-style. This is probably why I love what I do and don't mind the travel, facilitating meetings, and using my enthusiasm and energy to work with and through others. I have been using DiSC in my work with organizations for years, and it helps others to become more self-aware of their priorities and mindsets, which enables them to break down barriers when it comes to every organization's most important asset – the people!

The phone rang as the airline simultaneously texted me that our flight was taking off in an hour. This was awesome news!

I answered the phone, and it was my family inquiring about my flight status. I could see them all on FaceTime, which has made things so much easier. They were excited that I was coming home that evening, and I was excited to see them, too. I was blessed to have a strong star system to provide that ongoing support so I could do my best work as I helped humanize how organizations were enacting what they espoused to be important. And my family was a very important part of my support system.

I returned to checking my calendar. In the upcoming week, I was facilitating a health care system's sales team virtually from my home office, and then it was off to Boston for two large transformational meetings.

These meetings are important to me because they play an important role in cultural transformation. As an organizational development practitioner, the work I am doing has enabled me to make threads of connection between the three levels of leadership: the *individual, group,* and *organizational level.*

The upcoming meetings were the result of a small micro-intervention that has turned into a macro-organizational intervention, through the organization's leadership modeling the way, and encouraging the same behavior at the group level, while also encouraging individuals to embrace change and be transformational. This is what I love to see!

Following that, I would be delivering a keynote at a national conference for 400 individuals who were the recipients of a massive organizational cultural change initiative that is spreading like wildfire, making its way from the organization to the group level, or leadership teams, and now down to all the individuals within the organization.

Helping organizations optimize performance through their people is what I love to do. The return on investment is so worth it. There has been a huge *buzz* within the organizations I am working with, and differentiated behaviors are *taking flight*, which are transforming individuals and teams. The surrealness of these transformations makes me smile.

I checked the clock and let out a huge sigh. My flight would be leaving in 30 minutes. I was so excited to be heading home.

I have my family to thank for all of this work – none of which actually has anything to do with running my growing essential oil company. Sometimes I feel stretched thin and even overwhelmed, but my family is the *bees knees*, and I have them to thank for the impact I am making.

It is hard to imagine that the journey that brought me here began less than five years earlier with a simple family vacation to a farm.

CHAPTER 3

Be
Transfor-
mational

I was looking forward to my family vacation, which was a time for me to recharge from my busy life running a growing company, being a wife, and mom of two daughters, Lilly and Gabby. I had just celebrated my forty-third birthday on May 20, and while I felt blessed, something was weighing on me. The stresses of daily life are not uncommon for many families and the social media algorithms seem to have caught onto this, as it appears every video and meme I was seeing prompted a need for more coffee or a relaxing spa getaway. "A warm drink and a spa," I said dreamily, and closed my eyes.

Although my vacation would have little to do with the spa, the experience would be transformational.

I was just ready to sit down for 20 minutes to decompress from a long day when my kids yelled out, "Mommy, can you come downstairs? We want to talk to you." Just then, my cell phone pinged from my husband, Tom, who was apparently already down there. His text message forewarned me that the kids had an idea for our upcoming summer family vacation. I appreciated the heads-up, went downstairs, and hoped there was a spa.

Lilly and Gabby opened a PowerPoint, which was the last thing I wanted to see since running our growing company seems to be rife with presentations, but I sat down and got ready for the pitch. The first slide was a farmhouse. I cried internally, already thinking about how to respond. My kids apparently wanted to do a farm experience for our vacation! You heard that right. They wanted to spend over a week at a farm. Lilly and Gabby had what adults would call bucket-list items to do on the farm, but for my kids, it was their farmer-activity list. There was no spa listed in their PowerPoint.

It was super cute how they proposed this trip to my husband and me. They basically said they wanted to learn how to be more responsible and see what farmers' kids do to make them realize how great they have it! We both laughed, realizing how clever they are, and agreed they would probably end up in sales someday.

Their list was not long. It had one activity per day and left plenty of time for swimming in the property lake, playing sports, and relaxing as a family. They had the whole thing planned for our nine-day trip, which seemed like a very long time to spend on a farm.

The list included:

1. Milk a cow.
2. Shear a sheep.
3. Feed the pigs.
4. Go fishing.
5. Ride horses.
6. Feed the chickens.
7. Pick vegetables.
8. Enjoy flower gardens.

The girls made a compelling case, so it was off to H. Ives Family Farms with the entire family!

There was one thing weighing on my mind. Could I leave work behind? Our company, Essentially Proximal, was in the diffusing and essential oil business and was growing faster than it could adapt. Our mission to "cultivate a soul-nourishing experience through nature's beauty" had attracted a great team, but the growth was impacting the culture. We had people leave our company and tell us they felt less connected to our mission and values that we held so dear to our company – *recognition, reflection,* and *connection.*

While our family needed this time to get centered and recharge, I wanted to know if I could Be a Transformational owner of my company.

The Friday before we left for vacation, we had a townhall meeting with our entire staff, who were excited and overwhelmed by the growth of the company. This change and the recent attrition of managers left people feeling like this was not the company of the past. The townhall was mainly focused on reminding the company of our vision and our values, discussing the work that we did in serving our customers and making people feel happy and healthy by connecting them with nature's essential elements. I wanted the team to know that the company they joined was growing and changing for the better, and that we all play a role in ensuring the success of that growth and change.

Part of the townhall was a Q&A session from employees, so we could discuss any concerns that were on their minds. Sometimes people can be reluctant to speak up and voice their opinions. However, this townhall felt a little bit different; there was more engagement, more participation, more voices that hadn't typically been active in previous townhalls.

What I found illuminating is that people were expressing concern that they weren't sure that the company culture could remain the same. Leadership at all levels was focused on performance and not people, and our employees felt that our company values of recognition and connection were nonexistent between managers and employees. I realized it was the worst time to go away, but my family was looking forward to vacation, and I needed to prioritize this time.

I thanked the employees for sharing their experiences with us and assured them we would work to be better. I could sense their anxiety and stresses, so I followed the townhall with a separate meeting with our leadership team. I asked them to be mindful of how their teams and employees were feeling and, more importantly, to be ready to have some real transformational conversations upon return from our vacation.

CHAPTER 4

Be Present

The trip from our home outside Chicago to the middle of Iowa was about a six-hour drive. The kids had several games for the car ride, which kicked the vacation off with the right tone. The entire goal was to get connected as a family and spend time with the kids.

At the same time, I wanted to ensure our team at Essentially Proximal felt supported while we were away. It is not easy to disengage completely when you own your own business. In fact, many of the articles published on work-life balance talk about shutting everything down while on vacation. I am a firm believer in finding the balance and supporting both for me. I get energy from work!

We pulled into H. Ives Family Farms and were greeted by Helen Ives, the farm owner's daughter. Helen had the stereotypical farmer look. She was wearing black jeans, a cowgirl hat and T-shirt that said Be Friendly. She looked to be in her late 30s, and her dark hair was braided with a large yellow and black striped bow, reminiscent of my childhood. My husband told me she looked like Mary Ann from *Gilligan's Island*, but then quickly apologized with a wry grin. The reference reminded both of us that an island resort – with a spa – would have been my preferred choice for a vacation.

Gabby and Lilly jumped out of the car and said hello. I could see them wrinkle their little noses at the unfamiliar smell of the manure, cut grass, sweaty animals, and hay. Then they ran into the barn.

We were looking around for someone to help us with our bags when Helen said, "Hey ya'll, grab yourselves some of those wheelbarrows and throw your luggage in there. You can wheel them right this way to the front desk. My brother Levi will move your car."

Levi handed me a valet ticket. The large straw in his teeth was quite fitting. I handed him a token of appreciation, he tipped his hat, and quietly slipped the money into his dirty overalls as he slid into the driver's seat of our SUV. A farm with a valet? How curious, I thought.

My husband and I looked at each other and then the wheelbarrows. While the idea was clever, we saw that the wheelbarrows were likely used for other things in the past. As we placed our luggage in two wheelbarrows, my husband joked and said, "We are now the proud owners of 'pooie Vuitton' luggage."

I chuckled and said, "I thought the kids wanted to become more responsible." They were nowhere in sight as we pushed the wheelbarrows through the barn doors to the front desk, which was basically a barn door on two barrels. There was a stack of brochures on one end.

We stepped up to the front desk to a big "Howdy!" "I'm Beau! Welcome to the H. Ives Family Farms. The best farm in the land. I hope my cousin Levi took good care of you when you arrived!" he said.

My husband and I nodded and said it was wonderful.

Helen was smiling at Lilly and Gabby. They were feeding the chickens that were running around what appeared to be the lobby. Tom and I took a minute to soak in the girls' giggles and realized that this vacation was going to be an amazing experience for them. For us, we were unsure of how much we would get to relax and unwind, but seeing the kids' faces made everything feel right.

Beau checked us into one of the cabins on the farm. The cabin was equipped with a kitchen, fireplace, a couple of bedrooms (one with bunk beds), and a wraparound porch. The family room had a couch and some chairs. There were board games stacked neatly on a shelf under the coffee table. No TV, but thankfully Wi-Fi was included. I looked around for a bathroom and was delighted to find one. I had been envisioning *Little House on the Prairie* and having to use an outhouse and bathe in a horse trough. No spa, but the likelihood of a hot shower seemed promising.

The girls started picking out who would sleep where and Tom and I put the luggage in the rooms. Due to the kids' PowerPoint pitch, we had reserved all the activities in advance. Tomorrow we would be milking some cows. But we had today to ourselves to get the lay of the land.

We ventured outside to take in the atmosphere. It was quiet. It was peaceful. I could smell eucalyptus, which seemed to be coming from an herb garden not too far away. This was one of our best-selling oils.

We could see the lake, basically a large swimming hole, and a number of families were walking around the property. The girls wanted us to go down to the lake, so we all changed and made our way down the long path to the lake.

We had seen little John Deere tractors in front of the cabins, and we realized they were for the guests to get around the farm. Each tractor could hold four people, and all the families had theirs parked by the swimming hole. But we decided to walk the half mile, and our excitement to get there made the walk go by fast.

My kids made some immediate friends and were invited to join them on a big flower floating raft. It was Saturday, so work was quiet. As my husband sat and read a book, I opened my phone to check some emails. I found it therapeutic to make sure I was up to date on work. I responded to some emails but made it a point to schedule my send for Monday morning, so as not to disrupt anyone's weekend.

This balance was important for me; I truly believe one can be present at work and with family, while being mindful of how others may balance their work life. But this mindfulness was not translating as intended to our company culture, and the company's growing pains were keeping me up at night. Hopefully, I thought, I can get some rest, sleep in a bit, and do some soul-searching.

As I was crafting another email, the kids came running back to the chairs, dripping wet and begging for towels. I saved my draft and focused on them. It was time to Be Present with the kids and my husband. This was my commitment to the family – to balance the noise of life and enjoy every moment of memory making together!

CHAPTER 5

Be Curious

The rooster began crowing at 5:00 a.m. So much for sleeping in and being well-rested. There was nothing about a rooster in the brochure I had read about the farm, nor in the kids' PowerPoint presentation. Thankfully, I was an early riser, albeit this was about 45 minutes before I usually awoke.

I turned over to see if our new rooster friend woke my husband, too, but he had managed to bring his noise-canceling headphones. This led me to believe he had done some additional research about H. Ives Family Farms and failed to disclose the output of that research to me.

I was not worried about the kids. They sleep through anything, and also they stayed up past midnight last night. Actually, we all had. We played Uno and roasted s'mores and the girls ran around the farm with other children. The kids seemed much more interested in making friends than the parents did. The parents were outside on their cabin porches watching the kids run around while enjoying time with their significant other. The market lights strung between the trees lit up the pasture between all the cabins. The back of the cabins all faced the same direction, so it was easy to see the parents pretty much doing the same thing.

Normally, I would expect to see the soft glow of cell phones on people's faces in the darkness. Not here. It seems everyone was trying to Be Present last night.

This morning, I laced up my running shoes, unlatched the cabin door, and made my way down the path to the lake. It was dark out, but solar lights lit up the path, and I could hear the hustle and bustle of the H. Ives workers getting ready for the day. I started to run, and the strong smell of the farm was making me long to find that eucalyptus and herb garden I had smelled on the previous day. I had been running for about 15 minutes when I came across another well-lit path that took me in a different direction, away from the lake.

I decided to take the turn down this new road – it was beautiful. The trees and the smells were different. While I did not smell the eucalyptus, I did smell honeysuckle trees. It was lovely in the morning. I realized in that moment that we didn't have a honeysuckle essential oil line at Essentially Proximal, but we should have one. I couldn't help but think about our company for a moment – so much change – so many possibilities.

I usually ran about 3 miles every morning, and as I neared 1.5 miles, I prepared to turn around and head back to the cabin. The sun was beginning to rise, and I could hear the cows and goats in the distance. As I was making my turn, I saw a gentleman standing in the brush all decked out in what appeared to be a white hazmat suit. He had boots and gloves on, but his head was uncovered. He was lifting a thermos of what I assumed to be coffee to take a sip. I was not going to say anything, but he greeted me.

"Well, hello and good morning," he said.

I smiled and slowed down my pace and waved. I returned the greeting.

Trying to be funny, I said, "Is this some sort of biohazard area I've stumbled upon?"

I received a small chuckle. "No, Miss, you're in the best part of this farm," he said, before he took another sip of coffee.

I began jogging in place to keep up my heart rate. I try to get all the rings on my fitness watch to close on my watch each day, and I was not sure how long of a conversation this was going to be.

"Oh really?" I said. "Where am I?"

"Well, I am Henry Ives, the owner of the farm, and this is my sanctuary!"

"Oh, you're Helen's husband," I said. "I met her yesterday."

"Actually, Helen is my daughter," he said, "but thanks for the compliment."

Between the hazmat suit and the darkness, I did not realize this guy was so much older. I apologized and re-phrased my response.

"Well, your daughter is lovely," I said.

I realized it would be awkward to keep jogging at this point. My jog became a stand as my heartrate slowed.

"Thanks," he said, "She's a peach, for sure. How about joining me for a cup of coffee? Fresh brewed about 5 minutes ago."

He pointed to a small shed and a picnic table. I could smell the coffee and I decided to indulge. I was feeling the effects of the rooster.

"What's your name?" he asked me.

"Catherine with a C," I said.

He paused and the look on his face went from happiness to melancholy. He rebounded quickly and said, "That was my wife's name, too. What a fine name, and nice to meet you, Catherine."

I assumed the past tense in his response meant she was no longer with him. He poured me a cup of coffee, and I decided not to ask any questions regarding his wife. Fortunately, he started asking me questions. We talked about my family's vacation plans, the kids' activity list, and a bit about my company and what it did. He nodded and smiled, drank his coffee, and appeared to want to ask more questions, but I still had a burning question of my own. I wanted to ask him about his outfit.

"Henry, what is with the outfit you are wearing?" I asked. "And why did you say this is the best place on the farm – your sanctuary?"

"It looks like I've got a curious one on my hands," he said, as he put the coffee down. "Well, this here place is at the core of learning and growth," he said. "And this here white suit is a beekeeper's outfit. I guess it does kind of look like a hazmat suit," he said with a chuckle.

"The core of learning and growth?" I asked.

"You betcha!" Henry said. "Care to go on a bit of a walk with me?"

At first, I wanted to say no and get back to the kids, but then I thought of his late wife and the power of the universe. I was also curious about being at the core of learning and growth. I must have paused a bit longer than I wanted as I sorted out my response because Henry spoke again.

"You are not the slightest bit curious? Come on, Be Curious," he said.

I smiled and followed Henry down the path a bit further.

We came to the bee sanctuary, which was like an entertainment venue with a glass wall that peered out into a neighboring pasture where you could see a number of beehives in the distance. It looked like the venue was being prepared for an event. We entered into the huge, beautiful wooden cedar shed at one end of the sanctuary. I looked around and noticed a lone glass-enclosed beehive sitting toward the back of the shed where the bees could fly outside and back to the hive – but fortunately, they could not enter the shed.

This beehive, being glass, showed exactly what the bees were doing. I was amazed, and speechless; there must have been hundreds of bees in that hive. The bees were so active, and the honeycomb design was so intriguing. I wanted to tap the glass, like a kid in an aquarium, to see if I could get a reaction, but I tempered my childlike thoughts. I could see how the hive was operating, and right next to the hive was a table with some honey jars. I was in awe.

"Where are we?" I asked.

"This is my hive" he said.

"You're a beekeeper?" I asked.

"I am. And a farmer," he chuckled.

"This is remarkable. I have never seen anything like this. The honeycombs are so perfect, and there are so many bees!"

Just then my husband pinged my phone and asked where I was. I told him I was on a jog and was talking with Henry Ives, the owner of the farm. He told me to take my time; the kids were still sleeping, and he was going to read on the porch. This was perfect. Guilt-free curiosity, here I come!

"What are all these bees doing inside this hive?" I asked. "Did they build all that honeycomb?"

"They did build that honeycomb. In fact, bees are natural mathematicians. Bees create the honeycomb in a hexagon shape. It is the most efficient use of space in the hive; it utilizes the least bee resources, such as the wax that maximizes the honeycomb, and, interestingly, the hexagon shape stores the most honey," Henry said.

"Remarkable." I turned to look at Henry. "Do you sell honey here?"

"Well, we do sell their honey, but it is not the primary reason we have this hive. You see everything on this farm is the way it is because of these bees. The food you eat here, the flowers you see and smell, the grass for the horses and sheep, the lake – the bees take care of it all," Henry said.

Henry saw the puzzled look on my face. He walked me over to the hive and began to explain in more detail.

"You see, a healthy beehive functions as a well-oiled machine, thanks to tens of thousands of bees, performing their jobs dutifully. Bees function as a unit or team. Their workforce is capable of pollinating thousands of acres of flowering plants, producing upwards of 100 pounds of honey per year and continuously making new bees, so the hive can thrive."

That is so interesting, I thought. "Do bees always get along in the hive?" I asked.

"You see, Catherine, when everyone is focused on the same mission, they will all get along. Each bee has a very specific job and is not more important than the other. It reminds me of a quote from Harry S Truman, who said, "It is amazing what can be accomplished when we don't care who gets the credit." I believe bees function this way and collectively provide the nourishment required for all things to grow."

"What do you mean by jobs?" I inquired.

"I am glad I piqued your curiosity. I love talking about this with you, but I think I do have to get back to the bees and the farm. The guests are going to start lining up for their farm activities soon and I want to greet them with a smile. Are you planning to jog this way tomorrow? I'd be happy to answer your questions on how the many jobs of bees provides nourishment and enables the hive to thrive."

I nodded excitedly and said, "I will be back." Henry handed me a jar of honey from that table to take back to the family, along with one of those honey wands made of grooved wood. I thanked him for his time and, with a smile, ran back to the cabin.

On the run back, I kept thinking about what Henry said. **This place, the hive, is at the core of learning and growth, and bees provide the nourishment for all things to grow. Bees work together and are focused on the same mission.** I am so glad I was curious enough to follow Henry.

When I got to the cabin, I opened my laptop. On Friday, I had told my Essentially Proximal leadership team that I would check in and see if they needed anything and let them know how things were going. For my first message, I gave them a quote to think about. The email read:

Dear Leadership Team,

The hive is at the core of learning and growth, and bees provide the nourishment for all things to grow. Bees work together and are focused on the same mission.

—Catherine

CHAPTER 6

Be Nourished

At breakfast, I told my family about my encounter with Henry on my early morning run. The kids nodded in mild interest and said that it sounded cool, but they were more focused on the Sunday farm activities. My husband was more enthusiastic. Although he had studied finance and was the CFO of our company, he'd always had a creative side that many people didn't get to see. In fact, he's the one who came up with the name of our company, Essentially Proximal, which I love. "Proximal" means toward the center of the body and closest to the heart. That had always resonated with me – quite literally.

After breakfast, the entire family went to the barn where the cow-milking activity was set up for the kids. The girls started talking to their new friends; the parents all made a friendly gesture and acknowledgment of each other. Each family had a stool and some buckets with their name written on it. It was an adorable setup, and the girls were dressed in their farmer attire, pretty much resembling Helen, with their pigtails, black jeans and their cowgirl hats. I laughed to myself as I thought of that bow Helen had on when we first met resembling a bee. I realized it was not a coincidence and the universe was talking to me again.

The H. Ives Family Farm staff were great. They were jovial and energetic. The kids were all amazed. The staff showed the kids the proper way to milk a cow using a model that resembled the cows' udders. I had a chance to touch it, too. I think the point of this exercise was to get the kids comfortable with the technique so as not to upset the cows.

As the dairy cows entered, I could hear a child from another family refer to the Chick-Fil-A "Eat more chicken" slogan, which, as a business owner made me smile in appreciating "marketing gold" in action.

The farmers brought the dairy cow over to each family; there were five in total, and each family was responsible for filling their bucket with cow milk. With the assistance from an H. Ives worker, the kids were in their element. When the cow came to our stand, Lilly and Gabby were so enthused. They each took turns and were smiling joyfully and laughing.

This is *why* we are here, I thought.

The girls looked at my husband and me, standing behind them snapping pictures to capture memory-making in action. Lilly asked us if we wanted a try. As planned, my husband and I said "no thanks" in unison.

The H. Ives farmer assisting the girls chimed in. "Are you not the least bit curious how to milk a cow?" she said with a grin.

"Come on, Mommy and Daddy," the girls begged.

"Be Present and Be Curious," I thought to myself.

I sat down on the stool and my husband joined me on the stool next to me. It's a good thing we practice yoga, because the stool was seemingly designed for children and needed maximum flexibility to get into the sitting position.

The girls grabbed our phones and started snapping pictures and giggling. After we had our turn milking, all the families grabbed their milk and filled up a larger bucket. The staff took the bucket, and we followed them into a large room.

"This must be where the milk is made," Lilly said out loud.

The H. Ives staff worker smiled and said, "It most certainly is, but we don't produce too much cow milk here. We only have five female dairy cows on this farm, and their milk is used for you to enjoy. The butter, cheese, and even ice cream all come from these here cows."

"Fun fact," the friendly staffer said. "We also produce some of our bees' milk."

Everyone laughed. We all thought it was a joke. *Bees' milk – how silly.*

"Well folks, the cow-milking activity has come to an end, and you can all go about your day." Most of the families said thank you and left.

"Is there really something called bees' milk?" I asked.

"There sure is, miss; it is actually called royal jelly in the beekeeping community, but it looks like milk, so we call it bees' milk. The bees' milk feeds and nourishes the larvae in the beehive. It is a bit sour to human taste buds, but we do have some here. Would you like to try some?"

The girls nodded.

Just then, in walked Henry. My eyes lit up and I offered an awkward wave.

"Now this is your expert in bees' milk, if you have any questions" the H. Ives employee explained as they walked away with the bucket of milk.

"Henry, these young ladies would like to try some of the bees' milk."

"Wonderful!" Henry said.

The worker walked off with the bucket of cow's milk and waved goodbye over her shoulder.

Henry said, "Hello again, Catherine. This must be your family."

"Hello Henry, good to see you again. This is my husband, Tom, and our daughters, Lilly and Gabby," I said.

"How do bees make milk," Gabby asked?

"I see Gabby has her mother's curiosity, too!" Henry laughed. "Nice to meet you all. Well, I have a few moments to spare if you really want to know about bees and milk," Henry said.

We all looked at each other and nodded in agreement.

"Well, all right then. Follow me," he said.

We left the large room where they produced the cows' milk and entered a smaller room. It was about the size of an average bedroom, and it had a glass beehive like the one Henry had showed me in the morning. Henry asked us to put on some protective clothing so we could get closer to the hive and we all did with excitement.

Henry got down to the girls' level and changed his voice to engage them.

"You know girls, bees are fascinating creatures that come in many different shapes and sizes. Some bees you see flying around produce honey."

"We had honey this morning!" Gabby interjected.

Henry and I both looked at each other and smiled, because he knew it likely came from the jar that he shared with me.

"That is wonderful," Henry continued. "Other bees produce wax. But I bet you did not know that bees produce milk?"

We all shook our heads. We knew of beeswax, but not milk.

"Fun fact," Henry said. "Bees' milk is not dairy milk. Actual milk is produced by those dairy cows you met this morning or by our goats on the farm. Bees' milk is mainly made up of water with small amounts of sugar, proteins, and fat. Nevertheless, it is nutritious and quite enjoyable."

"Can we try some?" Lilly asked, looking up at us.

Henry led us over to a table. On the table was some honey and a small glass mason jar with a white liquid substance that looked like coconut milk.

"So I hear you are interested in tasting some of the bees' milk," Henry said.

"Sure," I said, as I laid my hand on Lilly's cute head. "During lunch, we can try some."

"How do you milk a bee without getting stung?" Gabby shouted in her most questioning voice. "Won't the bees sting you?"

The adults all laughed, as if a queue card was raised at a sitcom show prompting immediate laughter.

Henry said, "That's a fair question, and I bet Lilly was thinking the same thing." How kind, I thought, that he made sure Gabby did not feel like she said something no one else was thinking. He had a great way with kids.

Henry began pouring some bees' milk from the mason jar into small plastic disposable cups.

"Bees can produce milk through a process called 'bee lactation.' This is when bees make a substance from their belly that looks and tastes like the milk you tasted. **The hive must Be Nourished to continue to thrive, and the new bees that will soon be joining the hive environment must be ready to contribute to the hive's success.** The bee milk helps the new bees to grow big and strong so they can be productive bees. It can also be consumed by adult bees, like the queen, for her nourishment."

He handed each of us a cup and nodded to drink up. We all tilted the cups to our lips with hesitancy.

"Well, what do you all think?"

Our lips all pursed, and Lilly and Gabby said, "Sour!" in unison. We all put our cups on the table, and Henry laughed.

"Do all bees produce bees' milk?" I asked.

Henry smiled, realizing I was trying to get insights ahead of our upcoming one-on-one conversation about the jobs of bees.

"Not all bees make milk. Only the worker bees produce milk to fuel the growth of the hive with the bees' milk. It is fed to the bee larvae for three days, unless the worker bees choose a larva to be the queen, then they bathe that larva in bees' milk until the queen is born and they feed the bees' milk to her for the duration of her life."

"The worker bees are the ones who collect nectar and pollen from the proximal part of the blossom. They use this material from the heart of the flower to make honey and bees' milk is part of this process, too."

"Hey, proximal!" Gabby shouted. "That is Mommy and Daddy's company."

"Oh, is it? I didn't know that, Catherine. What a coincidence," Henry said with the tilt of his head. "The worker bees also build the honeycombs that you see here." He pointed to the hive we were standing around.

"You can see the worker bees caring for the larvae or new baby bees in the honeycomb. **Worker bees are all responsible for the success of the hive.**"

"And look, there is one of our queen bees!" Henry pointed and we all peered closer to the honeycomb.

"She lays the eggs and is responsible for the growth and development of the hive. The milk from the worker bees not only makes sure the baby bees can grow into big and strong, productive adult bees, but it nourishes the queen bee, who is responsible for keeping the hive growing and creating a productive environment."

"Similar to your role in your company, Catherine," Henry added. "What is it called?"

"Essentially Proximal," I said.

"Wonderful," Henry smiled and continued. "Essentially Proximal is your hive. You need the workers to produce at high levels, and ensure the new bees or employees are well trained and entering into a healthy and productive work environment. The reciprocity of how all the employees interact in the hive is important. Just as your employees need to Be Nourished, as queen bee, you need to Be Nourished, too. Ultimately, you are responsible for creating a healthy hive where your team can thrive. It is no coincidence that bees' milk has benefits to humans, especially when it comes to heart health and reducing stress and anxiety."

"Mommy, you're a queen bee!" Gabby yelled.

I smiled and recognized the importance of this example.

Henry gave us a little gift from his pocket. It was a packet of sunflower seeds. Not the ones you eat and spit out at the softball field, but a very special H. Ives Family Farms sunflower seed packet. He told us to find a place on the farm that has lots of sun and plant them there.

The girls were excited that we could choose the spot. He reminded us that bees will find the proximal part of the flower when it grows and use its nectar to pollinate the farm. This fuels the production of beautiful flowers, vegetables, and bees' milk, so H. Ives Family Farms too, can thrive.

As we walked out of the barn, the kids were happily skipping. We got lunch and took it down to the swimming hole to enjoy.

Throughout the day, I kept thinking about what Henry had said. While I am the queen bee, **I must make sure my people at Essentially Proximal can continue to**

Be Nourished. So, too, our people need to be a source of nourishment for others, so our company continues to grow and thrive.

I had been able to Be Present, Be Curious, and learn how important it is to Be Nourished today!

Before I went to bed, I opened my Essentially Proximal email and fired a quick note to the team. The email read:

Dear Leadership Team,

The hive must Be Nourished to continue to thrive, and the new bees that join the hive environment must be ready to contribute to the hive's success.

—Catherine

CHAPTER 7

Be
Vulnerable

Today was going to be a test. It was Monday. Essentially Proximal emails would be flowing in and group text notifications, while turned off, often cannot go ignored. My 5:00 a.m. feathered friend woke me up, but admittedly, I was tossing and turning all night long.

I kept questioning if I was creating an environment at Essentially Proximal that allowed for people to be nourished. Was the Essentially Proximal hive a source of nourishment for people, to build on Henry's analogy? I did not know, and, as queen bee, I was becoming worried.

I was looking forward to sitting down with Henry this morning. I became curious about his wife and wanted to ask him about Catherine.

As planned, I arrived at the hive where I first met Henry. He was not visible when I arrived, but I was about 10 minutes earlier than the previous day. It must have been my fast pace in anticipation to learn more from Henry. My mind was racing and apparently my legs were, too.

"What's on the agenda today with the kids?" a voice asked from down the path.

It was Henry.

"Oh, we get to shear some sheep today," I said.

"Well, isn't that something," Henry said. "The girls are going to love that. Come with me. I want to show you something."

Beyond the bee sanctuary, there was an open pasture with several grazing sheep. In the distance, through the soft glow of the rising sun, large white boxes were positioned around the pasture.

"You see them sheep over there?" Henry said. "They keep this pasture for me. When you all help shear the sheep today, you'll be keeping them healthy this summer." Henry explained that the sheep feed in the pastures all day and

49

night, effectively cutting the grass, which is important for allowing the outdoor hives to thrive. Henry said, "The sheep need the bees to continue to pollinate to ensure this pasture can grow. There are rich returns in the synergy between the bees and the sheep pasture.

"I'm part of that relationship, too. When you saw me yesterday, I was on my way out to the hives to check on them; that's why I was all decked out in my beekeeper suit.

"Now weren't we supposed to be talking about the jobs of bees?" Henry continued. "Before we start, I want to tell you that there are several different types of bees, and they all play a role in the hive colony. As the beekeeper, I am the shepherd of that colony, if that makes sense," he added.

I nodded. I could feel the first wave of emails vibrating in my phone as my mailbox synced up. Essentially Proximal was open. Let the day begin, I thought.

"You know how large this farm is, Catherine?"

I tried to recall the brochure, but nothing registered.

Henry pointed down and shook his finger, as if to show me something. We appeared to be standing in a large metal circle in the ground that looked sort of like a sundial.

"This area right here is the center; this sundial is the center of the farm. The heart of it all. One could say it is the proximal location of the farm."

I grinned and let out a curious gasp.

"This is the center of learning and growth. You see, the farm extends one and a half miles from this point. Do you know why, Catherine?" he asked rhetorically.

"It is because the bees generally travel up to three miles to feed and pollinate. So, when I opened it to the public on May 20, 1987, I wanted the bees to be pollinators of H. Ives Family Farms. The bees can travel in any direction and do what they do best. They always end up at the most proximal part of the farm. Right where we are."

"Hey, no kidding, May 20th is my birthday!" I said.

"Small world...what a coincidence," said Henry.

I nodded, remaining present and curious, realizing just how this time with Henry was nourishing to me.

"Bees fall into three main categories: worker, drones, and queens. Remember the bees' milk we talked about yesterday? When those worker bees are born and feed off all that bees' milk, they will grow into a bee called a forager. Sounds cool, right?"

Henry continued, explaining that forager bees receive the most recognition and the most prestige of all the bees in the hive, but it takes time for them to become forager bees. It takes growth and development of their mind and body! This is because the result of foraging is growth through pollination. Henry said, "It is one of the byproducts of hives that we all benefit from, Catherine. Bees encourage growth – all this green grass, flowers, food...and honey, of course!"

I was fascinated. I'd never heard of forager bees, but now I was learning that they are the hives' most valuable assets. A hive sends out those forager bees when they can protect themselves with a working stinger stocked with venom. Forager bees scour the three-mile radius from the hive looking for suitable nectar and pollen, then once their stomach is full and its pollen baskets are filled to the brim, a forager bee will return to the hive to drop off all the goodness it collected to one of its sisters.

Henry explained that the forager bees' work is never done. As quickly as it delivers goodies, it is leaving the hive again and, if that bright sun is shining, the forager bee will continue until it grows weary. Foraging is one of the last duties a worker bee will perform for the hive; it will work until it collapses from exhaustion.

"Wow!" I said, shaking my head. I had no clue how important worker bees were to the hive and pollination.

"Working is their job, and they give everything to the hive. **They support the growth and development of the hive and pollinate the environment to nourish the environment around them**," Henry said.

This is remarkable. "What do drone bees do?" I asked. "They sound cool."

"Honestly, drones have a reputation of being lazy and ride the coattails of the more productive bees in the hive. Drones don't carry their weight in the hive, but they are integral to the lifecycle of the bee. While they don't make honey, they will certainly indulge in eating it. Protecting the queen or the hive in not a priority for the drone. Their main job is to mate and spread their genes to neighboring queen bees. The hive needs drones for the greater survival of the species."

Henry smiled and looked me in the eyes. "And finally, that brings us to the queen bee, Catherine. As we know, the queen bee's job is crucial. She ensures the future population of the entire hive. She lays up to 2,000 eggs a day, choosing the exact spot in the hive to lay them and how many of each type (worker or drone eggs) to produce. For most of her life, aside from mating, she lives in the hive and runs the hive. She can live two to five years."

We walked back to the cedar shed to see the hive in action. Henry pointed out the different types of bees. You could easily spot the drones. They looked larger and lazier than the worker bees.

I looked at my watch and realized I needed to get going to the sheep-shearing activity. I thanked Henry and told him I wanted to hear about his wife, Catherine, sometime. He nodded. He told me that he would not be able to meet me tomorrow morning because he had an errand to run but would welcome more conversation before I left the farm.

We parted ways and I jogged back to the cabin. Along the way, I thought about the types of bees and how they related to Essentially Proximal. Was my leadership team acting like forager bees, pollinating the environment with goodness and transforming it?

I wondered if we had more drones at Essentially Proximal; there were definitely some employees that spread the good vibes at our company and lived the mission and values, but there were others who just cluttered the hive and provided little value.

Later that morning, as our family listened to the farmer telling us about sheep shearing, the girls sat in awe. The families gathered around us were different from the previous day, but the girls' new friends were still there, and the children all giggled when one sheep let out an indignant "baaaaaa!" Assuming more people came to the farm over the weekend, I was delighted that the Monday crowd was not as busy.

The farmer explained that the sheep go out to pasture and eat the grass, keeping it well-manicured. "The wool from these sheep will be used to make some fine blankets and clothes one day, but that's not why we're shearing them now. Summers are hot, and here at H. Ives Family Farm we want our sheep to feel great." The farmer explained that feeling great both physically and mentally is the key to growing – for sheep and humans! "These grazing sheep will be very grateful to have their wool removed so they can freely go about and eat the green grass."

"Now," the farmer asked, "Who wants a turn shearing?"

At first, the kids were a little reluctant, feeling scared they would hurt the sheep, but when the farmers assured them that the shears were safe and the sheep would be fine, their faces lit up with excitement.

All the kids had a chance to shear part of the sheep wool. The sheep made their "baa" sounds; it was quite fitting.

When the shearing was finished, the sheep stood up and looked completely naked. All the kids laughed and said it looked funny.

The farmer chuckled too, but then he rubbed his hand across one of the sheep and told the kids, "This here sheep, while bare, will get a chance to grow a new coat and feed in pastures this summer. **Regrowth and rebirth are at the core of learning and growth**," he said.

He said that sometimes it's good to Be Vulnerable in front of others. **Showing vulnerability in front of a group opens the door for more authentic conversations.** We shouldn't laugh at someone when they are trying to be bare. "After six months," he said, "this sheep will feel and look great, with a new coat of wool. Sheep and people aren't so different. If we keep letting our wool grow without being bare, we may never get to experience growth and rebirth."

I wasn't sure the kids were following this learning point, but I think the message resonated with the parents.

That evening, after all the fun and activities were done, the girls stayed in the cabin and watched the *Bee Movie* on their tablet. It was a lovely night, so my husband and I went for a walk. We reflected on the day and talked about work and emails that had come in.

When we returned, I sat down at my computer and shared another quote with my leadership team. The email read:

Dear Leadership Team,

Be Vulnerable with your team. This will accelerate your personal growth. Like the forager bee, you'll also pollinate the environment around you, providing the fuel needed for others to grow.

—Catherine

CHAPTER 8

Be Messy

On Tuesday, I decided not to go for my run. Instead, I sat outside by the lake and did some yoga. That is one thing the farm was missing – yoga and Pilates classes. The sun was rising over the horizon, and it felt so peaceful.

The smell of the farm was becoming more natural. When I finished my yoga poses, I grabbed my phone to take a picture of the sunrise and saw an email come through from Essentially Proximal. It was from someone on the leadership team, and it read:

> Loving the quotes. Thanks for sharing. I hope you're enjoying your vacation and refueling. We won't leave any messes for you to clean up when you get back.

Messes, I smiled to myself. Considering what our family was about to do before breakfast, I thought it was an appropriate word.

Today, we were feeding the pigs. The note from our activity's coordinator said not to wear anything that you were not willing to get dirty. We had packed outfits specifically for this, so old clothes, and sneakers it was!

As we walked to the pig pen, the kids could not stop talking about the *Bee Movie*. They were talking about how bees pollinate everything, and they were excited to see the flowers while we were here. The movie was a hit and I quickly realized that bees were all the rage this trip.

We arrived at the pig pen. Literally, that is what it is called. You could see the pigs behind a gate, and they looked eager to eat.

The farmer explained to us that the farm used the leftover food from the cafeteria for the pigs. We were grateful to receive rubber gloves as farm workers rolled in massive garbage cans full of food scraps. The farmer explained that we are going to have a competition. The first family to fill their trough and empty their garbage could open the gate and let the pigs in. Of course, Lilly and Gabby looked up at us with a competitive twinkle in their eyes. We knew this meant we had better win.

The farmer said, "On your marks, get set, go."

All the families grabbed a handful of food and started filling the trough. It was so gross, but the kids were having fun.

Unfortunately, our family did not win, but the kids had a blast. The farmer let the family who won open the gate and the pigs ran in and started eating. The "oink" sounds were so cute.

Then the farmer unexpectedly hit a big red button on the wall and more food started filling the troughs from an automatic feeder. We were all a little startled.

"You didn't think we feed the pigs with a food waste contest every meal, did you?!" The farmer chuckled and said that this farm is highly automated, but they wanted us all to get a glimpse of how to feed the pigs.

After we hosed off, we all gathered around to watch the pigs eat. The farmer explained that while pigs are known to Be Messy, they live a great life. He explained that just because we think the process of feeding a pig is messy does not mean that it is not important.

"The meat from these pigs feeds many people and is part of the food chain. The food you fed them was all grown right here on the farm – pollinated by the beehives."

He asked, "Does anyone know why pigs rolled in the mud?"

Lilly, of course, shouted out, "The pigs love to get dirty and play with their friends!"

The farmer said it was certainly fun to play in the mud, but there was a different reason. "Pigs play in the mud to cool off. The mud prevents them from overheating when it is hot outside. It is even better than the water."

The farmer said, "You know, we're not so different from the pigs. For us, too, **there are a lot of times life gets messy, and we need to find creative ways to cool off and continue to flourish."**

The farmer pointed to one of the beehives. He told us that unlike the pig pen, bees take responsibility to clean their hive. Cleaning bees are the type of worker bees that remove dead bees and clean out the honeycomb, so the queen can lay new eggs. Hives are one of the most naturally sterile environments.

The farmer said, "The pig pen is not so sterile." Everyone laughed.

We spent the rest of the day together. We went to the lake and had an amazing picnic. As I was checking emails, I saw that one of the leaders had shared a quote I sent with his team. I was copied in on the email, and it made my heart smile. I showed my husband, and he smiled, too.

As I was going through my email, I shared another quote:

Dear Leadership Team,

There are a lot of times life gets messy and we need to find creative ways to cool off and continue to flourish.

—Catherine

I spent the remainder of the day thinking about how I need to roll in the mud sometimes and cool off. The recognition that it is OK to Be Messy was a humbling reminder that nothing is perfect.

CHAPTER 9

Be Patient

I took my Wednesday morning run by the proximal part of the farm, hoping to see Henry. I took a longer route today, as I wanted to get a good workout in.

This was our day to go fishing. We were not a fishing family. In fact, I was pretty sure we had never gone fishing, as a family, ever. Between running the business and the kids, we just never made time for it.

I thought Tom was OK with it, though. He seemed to enjoy all the girls' activities with soccer and tennis. They were quite active in sports, which kept him busy. And he still found time to occasionally go golfing.

I wasn't so interested in fishing, but I loved being on the water, so the fishing trip was likely to be more of a boat trip for me. The lake that we were going to was different from the swimming hole, and I thought it would be a nice getaway.

My thoughts about fishing evaporated as I arrived at the sundial and stared into the pasture. I saw the sheep grazing, and they were all bare. They looked refreshed and ready for the summer.

I followed the path past the pasture where I had not ventured before. I arrived at a beautiful garden. Its entrance had one of those bougainvillea arches over a stone path. Bird feeders adorned the trees, and several bird baths were positioned around the garden. I could smell fresh honeysuckle, and the air here seemed crisp. I walked further down the path, and my senses were heightened as one of my favorite scents, lavender, was in the air. I spotted a nice bench. This was such a zen spot to relax. The bench had an engraving on it, and I leaned closer to read the inscription:

"To my Catherine. I will patiently await the time we can see each other again. Please be patient and wait for me. I will tend to our hive. You are my queen bee."
Henry

My vision blurred as my eyes filled with tears. It was like a Hallmark movie moment, where you try but cannot hold back the tears. It was such a beautiful tribute to his wife.

I left the garden and ran back to the cabin. I did not see Henry but was excited for our family fishing adventure today.

The brochure had suggested we take the tractor to the lake, as it was about three-quarters of a mile away from the cabins. We all hopped on the tractor and headed to the lake. There was only one boat tied to the dock when we arrived. The side of the boat was painted with a bold black border, and a name in black and yellow stripes: *Catherine's Bee V*. We assumed that was our ride, so my husband and I walked along the shore while the kids took off running, chasing ducks.

We stood by the boat and looked around, and then heard a jolly "Ahoy!"

"Well, fancy meeting you folks here," said the voice.

It was Henry! He was walking toward us with a small tool in one hand and his thermos in the other. "You mind if I captain your ship today?" Tom and I nodded; the girls ran back to our side, yelling, "Yay! It's Henry!"

Henry had the poles and tackle ready to go. He told us that there were a few types of fish in this lake, including large and smallmouth bass, bluegill, and catfish.

He asked us if we had fished before, and we all shook our heads, no.

"Fishing requires you to quiet your mind and Be Patient. Nothing is more important in fishing than to surround yourself with nature and just wait."

Henry explained that when we toss the hook into the lake with a live wiggle worm, we want to watch the bobber. The bobber will float to and fro, moving with the flow of the water and bobbing up and down. We must carefully watch the bobber, because when the bobber starts to go under water, there is probably a fish nibbling on the line. You might be tempted to start quickly reeling it in, but if you do, you're likely to lose the fish. Instead, you want to let the fish take a good bite to set the hook. Then you can gently reel it into the boat. Henry warned, "I can tell you, if you try to reel the line in too early, without setting the hook, the fish will be gone – likely with your worm."

Henry showed us how to bait the hook and cast the line. Equally as important, he taught us to Be Patient out in the hot sun.

My husband caught the first fish, a bluegill, and the girls were so happy and excited at the prospect of catching one themselves.

Gabby saw her bobber dip and shouted, "Next!" She tried to reel in the line very fast, but it became tangled up in the reel. When she realized there would be no fish, she became frustrated and started to cry.

"That's OK there, Gabby," Henry said. "This is fixable."

"How?" she asked. "The line is all tangled."

"Well, let's take a look," he said, "You've got yourself in a little pickle, but there's a couple of solutions to consider. We could cut the line and start over, or we can untangle the mess and try to understand what happened, so it does not happen again. That will take longer, Gabby, but I will leave the decision up to you. Would you like a quick fix, or do you want to be patient and try to understand what happened to the line so it does not happen again?"

Gabby looked at Lilly and her dad, who were still fishing. We all looked at Gabby. She said, "Can we try and untangle the knot to understand what happened?"

Henry and Gabby spent almost 15 minutes working out the knot. Fifteen minutes normally seemed like forever to her, but she took the time with Henry to see how to untangle the knot. As they worked together and talked, she learned that the faster she reeled, the more likely the line would get caught in the spinning reel and make a big mess. Thus, she needed to slowly reel the line in to prevent this.

"Aha!" Henry smiled. "That's it. The line is fixed. I am proud of you for being patient. Let's bring our lines in, everyone; we are going to take the boat around the corner." Henry turned on the motor and after a quick 10-minute drive, we saw a new part of the lake.

"Lilies!" Lilly exclaimed.

"That's right," said Henry. "We love lilies here at the farm."

"Wow!" I said. "The colors are amazing!"

"These vibrant colors attract our honeybees," he said.

"The main goal of honeybees is to produce honey for the queen and all the new baby bees. To do that, they need a lot of nectar and pollen. Lilies are rich in nectar and pollen.

"Lilly," he asked, "Are you full of the good stuff, like these here lily pads, that makes people grow?"

She nodded, feverishly.

"Well, these pollen-rich lily flowers help fulfill the bees' need for protein, which is required to make all that yummy honey. They'll spend their entire trip on one type of flower and cross pollinate all the lilies."

Just then, a breeze carried the strong fragrance of the lilies to our boat and made us smile.

"OK," Henry said. "Let's cast out those lines and try to catch one of them big fish."

We all cast out, including me, and waited. It was so peaceful...

Until...Gabby shouted, "I got one!"

I actually heard myself coaching her, like a pro. "Remember your lesson while you were practicing patience, Gabby. Reel the line in slowly. Let the fish come to you." As I watched my daughter pull and reel, her face concentrating on her prize, I realized her struggle had a bigger lesson: **Don't let something pull you down, causing you to get all tangled up. There are rich returns when you can be patient.**

Just then, the fish jumped. It was a whopper of a bass. Gabby managed to pull the fish close to the boat, and with the help of her father brought the fish in the boat. It was beautiful. We snapped a picture and called it a day. Henry added it to the fish basket. The boat ride back was peaceful.

The purr of the motor pushing through the water lulled the girls to sleep. My assumptions about the lakes connecting were confirmed, as we moved easily from one small body of water to another.

I asked Henry about all those colorful red plants that lined the lake.

He laughed and said, "Would you believe they are impatiens?"

He said, "If you want to get to the peaceful lake, first you have to get through the impatience (a play on words of course). Then you can practice Being Patient.

"You can find patience in the proximal part of the lake – closest to the center where the bees get their nectar from the lily pads and the fuel they need to make things grow."

As the boat pulled up to the dock, the kids stirred from their nap. We thanked Henry.

I did not mention that I saw his special garden, with the engraved bench. Bringing that up somehow felt too personal with the entire family there. If there was one thing that was a consistent theme today, it was to be patient. I would ask him another time.

The rest of the day flew by. We ended up going to bed early, as the sun had taken a lot out of us.

I opened the laptop to a flurry of emails. I read them all and responded. They all seemed to have the same theme today; people were waiting for responses from others before they could do their job. I responded to every email the exact same way. It read:

Dear Leadership Team,

Don't let something pull you down, causing you to get all tangled up. There are rich returns when you can be patient.

—Catherine

CHAPTER 10

Be Calm

On Thursday morning, the family was planning to go on a trail ride. We had been petting and feeding some of the lovely horses over the course of the week, and the girls already knew the ones they wanted to ride.

I told them I was not actually sure if they would get their choice, but they had high hopes. Like many of the activities on the farm, this would be a first for our family. None of us had ever been on a horse. My husband wasn't looking forward to this outing, but as with most activities, the kids were super pumped.

When we arrived at the stable, Levi greeted us. We recognized him immediately as the man who had valeted our car. He was pretty much wearing the same thing.

My husband, as usual, tried to be funny and asked Levi if he was in charge of transportation at the farm.

"Anything that gets people around, I handle," Levi said with a chuckle.

Levi asked everyone to gather around the stable. There were about 12 people, kids and adults, going on the trail ride. Everyone seemed to be giving off the same vibe. They were both excited and nervous. Levi asked, "Who here has ridden a horse before?" Three hands went up.

He said, "Well, you're in luck. These horses do trail rides all day long. They could walk the trail in their sleep. I'm going to pick out a horse for each of you based on your size."

He proceeded to easily mount a horse and brought it around to the front of the group. The horse tail was whipping around like a flyswatter because Levi had failed to see a nice pile of steamy horse droppings the horse was standing over. The fly community was taking full advantage of it.

"We will help you mount your horse. Once you're on, hold onto the reigns. The horse will stay quite still. If you want the horse to move right, you move the reigns right. To go left, you move them left. If you want to stop, you gently pull back and say, 'Whoa.'

Levi said, "Can I get a 'Whoa' from the group?" Everyone said "Whoa!" at the same time, quite harmoniously.

"To get the horse moving, you need to make a clicking sound with your mouth and give the horse a gentle tap with your heel. Let me show you."

Levi made the click-click sound with this cheek. He asked us all to try. You could imagine what it sounded like when 12 people try to all click at the same time – not quite as harmoniously as when we had said "Whoa!" The horses all looked up as if to laugh.

The farm helpers retrieved the horses from their stalls, each leading two horses at a time. Levi got off his horse and came to the group. He helped us up onto the horses as the farm hands held them. They continued to hold the horses until everyone was mounted and Levi got back on his horse.

The entire group was quiet and listening. We were all focused on Levi, and you could sense that there was quite a bit of anxiety as we waited for what would come next.

He said, "OK, now we are going to be single file and head out. The ride will take 30 minutes. Once we get to our location, we will dismount and feed and water the horses and have a nice snack ourselves."

"Is everybody ready? Let's go!" he said, and off we went.

We started down the tree-lined, sun-kissed trail. It was wide enough for two horses to comfortably walk side by side, but we stayed in single file. When I had a chance to glance at my girls, I saw how the light painted a nice glow on their faces. Levi led the way, followed by the rest of the group, me, Lilly, Gabby, and then my husband. About 10 yards behind us were two farm hands riding side by side. I guess they were the safety patrol.

"Whoa!" I heard from the front of the line. We all gently pulled the reigns. Everyone was pointing up and looking in the trees. Beautiful natural beehives hung high up in the trees. It was remarkable. They were so different from the wooden beehive boxes I had seen in the sheep pastures. These natural works of art looked like some sort of Chihuly glass sculpture. We all clicked and gave our horses a heel to get them going again.

Up ahead, we could see an opening that looked to be the trail's end.

Just then I heard a "Whoa, Whoa, Whoa, now!" from the rear. My husband's horse was jumping around and neighing. The farm hands from the back raced up.

My husband looked a bit panicked as he tried to stay on. One of the hands made his way to the front, as Levi moved toward the back.

"Be Calm!" he yelled. "No need to pull the reigns that hard or fight against the horse. Horses sense fear and anger. It makes them nervous. Calm yourself."

My husband said "whoa" more calmly and rubbed the horse neck. The horse stopped shaking its head vigorously and swatting its tail. "Whoa there, whoa there," my husband repeated, more calmly. His heart was racing, but his voice started to steady. The girls looked scared for their dad, but it was all fine. After the scare, we proceeded to make our way to the end of the trail.

I could not believe my eyes. It was a beautiful picnic area with horse troughs, feed, and carrots for the horses, along with picnic tables laid out with trays of fruit, bottles of water, and some cold towels.

We dismounted our horses with the assistance of the farm hands, fed the horses a carrot and sat down at a table. The field was beautiful, the grass was green, and dandelions and small white flowers peppered the field. You could see some sheep in the distance. I bet those bees we saw played a role in this beauty, I thought to myself.

As our family was getting a chuckle at the table about scared daddy, Levi came by. He sat down and asked if everyone was OK. My husband nodded yes and said the horse just started whipping around and he did not know what to do.

Levi said "Horses, like many animals, have the ability to sense anxiety and fear. Horses can sense fear in any animal. Some call it an instinct, but according to some scientists, emotions – particularly strong ones – give off a scent. They call these *pheromones,* and they can be smelled by any animal and by some humans."

"Phermose," Gabby said. "No. Pheromones," Lilly corrected. "Ohhh, phermones," said Gabby.

Levi continued, "Remember how you saw me walk up and quickly mount my horse, and the horse was accepting of that. There is a reason that happens, though. It's the pheromones that I exude. Horses can smell the pheromones of love, joy, and happiness. They can also sense anger and sadness."

"Hey, like the *Inside Out* movie," Gabby said. She reminded us of the Disney movie about the role emotions play in humans.

I nodded and smiled at Gabby.

"Haven't seen that one," said Levi, "but sounds like a dandy!"

"So, I was giving off nervous or scared pheromones," said my husband.

"Yes. Something probably spooked the horse and then you got nervous and gave off those pheromones. But when you rubbed the horse, demonstrating love and nurturing it, the horse calmed down. You gave of a different type of pheromone," Levi said.

My head immediately went to Essentially Proximal. I felt this in the room with my leaders after the townhall. I sensed their anxiety and fears. Was this their pheromones?

But then a new possibility occurred to me: Diffuse the pheromones. The company was always looking for innovative ideas, and I was not sure if anyone had already cornered the pheromone diffusing market, or if it was even possible.

Half-joking, I said, "We should bottle those pheromones up and sell them."

"They already sell bottled pheromones," said Levi. "You can buy pheromones to calm nervous horses by rubbing them on."

My husband pulled out his phone and made a couple of quick notes. I smiled, realizing my idea might have some potential.

"I bet the horse got bit by one of those bees in that cool hive we saw," said Gabby.

"Funny you say that!" Levi said. "Just like horses, bees can smell fear, and they have an excellent sense of smell. They can use their sense of smell to avoid danger and to protect their hives. When a single bee in the hive senses an emotion like anger, frustration, or fear, it can easily communicate with the others so that the whole hive is quickly informed and can protect itself. It is all about keeping the hive safe and thriving."

"That is why we want to give off the pheromones of love and joy," Gabby said.

We laughed, as Levi stood up and made the announcement that it was time to mount up and head back. This time, my family was at the front of the line, right behind Levi.

As we took the trail back, I stared at the trees. Everything that mattered seemed to keep coming back to the bees. I looked for those works of art in the trees. I wanted one last look of the hives that were created by these amazing bees – not one that was man-made, but created by the bees themselves, in their vision, with the resources from nature. It took me back to our Essentially Proximal vision: "Nature's beauty."

We enjoyed the rest of the day by the swimming hole. This was turning out to be better than a resort spa vacation. I took a dip in the lake, played with the kids, and was present in the moment.

We decided to stay at the swimming hole until sunset. They were bringing out sparklers and other activities for the kids. My husband was napping, I was at peace.

I shot a quick message to the leadership team before the end of the day. It read:

Dear Leadership Team,

Be calm in times when the environment around you may be causing anxiety or stress. People can sense when something is off and may communicate those feelings to others, causing an unwanted ripple effect.

—Catherine

CHAPTER
11

Be

Challenging

On Friday morning, I got up early. I wanted to go back to the spot where we saw all the hives yesterday to take pictures. I packed a backpack with my good camera, which was much better than my phone camera because it has a powerful zoom lens that allows me to get some really nice shots! My husband was just getting up when I left but the kids were still sleeping, so I let him know my plans.

I figured it was early enough that a trail ride would not be happening, so I jumped on the tractor that got us around the farm and headed toward the stable. Dew was covering the grass and the sun was just rising. When I arrived at the stable, the horses were grazing outside. I spotted my horse. I remembered his name is Larry, which seemed like a random name for a horse, but he seemed to like it. I stopped the tractor and went over to the fence. I started clicking and said, "Here, Larry!" click click, "Here, Larry!"

Larry was a pretty lazy horse; he didn't even lift his head. I tried one more time – actually I cupped my hands around my mouth and called out, "LARRRYYYY, HERE LARRY, HERE LARRY." I was reenacting the scene from *Annie*, where she used that tactic to try to prove to the dog catcher that Sandy was her dog. Remarkably, Larry lifted his head and began to slowly walk over to me. I let out a "Good Ole Larry," which was Annie's response in the movie when her call succeeded.

I rubbed Larry's nose and face and gave him a pet. He was still chewing on hay from the field. I kept petting him. I knew the pheromones I was emitting were love and affection. I soaked up the peaceful sights – Larry, the dew-covered field. This was bliss.

"Whoa!" I heard someone say. I turned around and it was no other than Henry, riding into the stable.

"Good morning," I said with a smile. "Was I giving off some pheromones that made you feel that I was a warm and accepting person?"

Henry laughed. "Well, Larry seems to think so. What brings you out this way so early? And you decided not to jog? Looks like you took the trusty tractor. Are you in a hurry?"

"No, I'm not in a hurry at all. I was planning to head down to the trail and get some cool photos of the natural beehives we saw on the trail ride. I brought the tractor so I could get away in case the bees started sensing danger," I said kind of sheepishly.

"Well if you're up for it, I can saddle up your friend Larry and we can head that way together."

I nodded. I never turned Henry down, because he always brought me such wisdom – and I was a Be Curious type of person lately. As Henry saddled up Larry, I asked him how he had been, and we caught up. I texted my husband and said that I was down by the stable and saw Henry and he offered for me to ride Larry again. My husband sent me a question mark, and a confused emoji. After I re-read the text I understood why, as I am not quite sure he remembered my horses name was Larry. I provided clarity to him with a heart emoji, and he sent me a thumbs up.

Henry and I began our casual stroll down the trail, side by side. He asked how the company was holding up and we chatted about what I was going to do when I get back with the leadership team. I told him that a pressing question weighed on my mind: How was I going to be transformational for Essentially Proximal?

Henry offered some words of wisdom and talked about his farm being a family. He was careful to hire people who had the same values to become part of the family. He passed on to the new employees the rich traditions from when the farm started that had made the H. Ives Family Farm a success. He also gave each employee a book with blank pages so they could author their own story as they build their new traditions.

I absolutely loved this! He was giving me so many ideas.

Henry slowed down and called his horse to a stop so I followed suit. He pointed up to one of the natural beehives in the trees. Just as it had the day before, it reminded me of a Chihuly glass sculpture.

I dismounted Larry and got out my camera. I began to snap some of the most amazing pictures I had ever taken. As I zoomed in, I could see that the bees on the hive never seemed to rest. I stopped shooting for a moment and just used the zoom lens as binoculars, observing the bees. I tried to locate the queens, drones, and worker bees.

"Everything OK?" Henry asked.

"Yes," I replied. "I am just studying them. It appears all the bees are just working together perfectly in their hive. No issues in the hive, just harmony."

Henry said, "Follow me. I'll show you something else."

I took a few last photos and got back on Larry. We walked toward the fields where the group had taken a break on our trail ride on Thursday. Before the entrance to the field, Henry stopped.

He said, "Catherine, you see this hive up there in the tree?"

I nodded.

"Take a look at the ground. What do you see?"

"Looks like some dead bees and some honeycomb fragments" I replied. Basically, it looked like little pieces of Honeycomb cereal on the ground.

"Now take out your camera and get some pictures of that hive," he said.

While it wasn't the prettiest hive, I took out my camera. I zoomed in, and saw a bunch of bees swarming around the hive. This was not something I had seen. I kept observing.

"What do you see?" Henry asked.

"The bees are swarming all around. Why?" I questioned.

"You mentioned you see harmony in the hives, collaboration, and support. This hive here has been infiltrated by another colony looking to steal its honey. There is fighting going on between the bees."

Henry said that a weaker hive becomes a target for robbing, for any of several reasons. Maybe there is a nectar shortage, and those things that provide bees the fuel for growth is limited. When one hive cannot find a source of nectar to drive growth for the hive, the hive sends out scouts and then preys on the weakness of another hive. They've discovered the intruders, and now there's a real battle going on. A weaker hive becomes a target for robbing. That essentially renders it useless.

"This is so interesting, Henry. It is akin to a company not being able to find sources of growth for their organization, so they go out and find the growth drivers at other companies. I am seeing this now at Essentially Proximal. People are leaving for other companies. Am I not providing the internal nectar for my hive?"

"Well, Catherine. It sounds like you are trying to make threads of connection, which I appreciate."

Nodding, I asked Henry, "Is robbing the only way bees become aggressive and fight?"

"Actually, no. There are other factors like weather and humidity, but the most important factor, in my opinion, to a bee's aggressiveness is a queen-less hive. In the absence of a queen, the bees have no direction, and they become feisty. But as soon as a new queen steps in and regains control of the hive, the bees' behaviors change."

I put my camera away and got back on Larry. Henry suggested we give the horses some water, so we finished our ride to the field and let the horses drink. We sat on a bench and looked out into the field of grass from yesterday with the dandelions and flowers.

I told Henry how pretty it all looked – all the yellow and white flowers.

"Indeed," he said. "It is a lovely sight. These are the prettiest weeds around."

I felt him giving out friendly, engaging pheromones, so I said, "Weeds? They look like flowers to me."

"Well plants, flowers, and the bees have been able to find a way to evolve together. Most people try to nip the weed problem in the bud, pardon my pun," Henry chuckled. "But here at the farm, we welcome these weeds because they play a role in the growth of all this beauty around us, even if many people don't understand."

"What do you mean?" I asked.

Henry said that people assume that the weeds and the other plants compete for nutrients in the soil, so they try to kill the weeds. However, the weeds' nectar is an equally important source for pollination. We need weeds to Be Challenging the flowers and other plants in the field. When there is healthy conflict between a weed and a plant, the plants can grow to be even more resilient and productive. "The weeds' and the plants' existence are intertwined so intricately that one without the other may struggle to survive."

"Are you saying we need weeds in our life?" I asked.

"Weeds can help us grow, too." On the surface, Henry explained, weeds seem like a nuisance. But, when we learn how to manage them correctly, they can actually fuel growth in the environment.

"Honestly, Henry I spray poison on my weeds to get rid of them quickly and kill them." This was quite a different perspective.

"Don't get me wrong, Catherine; there are weeds that are unhealthy for the surrounding environment. Some weeds can even take over the environment. You must get rid of those weeds. But we need to remember that, while weeds can be a challenge, they offer value in fertilizing soil and attracting beneficial insects."

I thanked Henry again for his insight. We mounted our horses and headed to the stable. I petted Larry and said goodbye. I could see a group of people in the stable getting ready for the morning trail ride. Levi came over and hugged Henry. "Good morning," he said.

"Good morning, Levi!" I responded.

Henry told Levi to give Larry a rest today, as he had just had a ride. I said goodbye to them, hopped on my tractor, and went back to the cabin.

When I arrived, my husband asked if Larry was worth the ride. I smiled and said I had a great time.

I sat down at my laptop and crafted an email to the leadership team at Essentially Proximal. It read:

Dear Leadership Team,

Challenge the status quo with intent to make us better. It is OK to take a questioning and skeptical lens. Other companies might try to steal our talent, but we should create an environment where they are not leaving because of our leadership.

—Catherine

CHAPTER 12

Be Energizing

Today, we were going to the chicken coop to collect eggs. Our family eats eggs all the time. In fact, the girls had recently let us know that they preferred egg whites, and since that's healthier, we were happy about their newfound attention to nutrition.

The chicken-coop activity was something the girls really wanted to do. We had scheduled this for early afternoon, and decided to invest the morning with a walk around the farm. I took Tom and the girls to the proximal part of the farm. I began explaining to them that from this spot, the farm extends a mile and a half in every direction, so the forager bees can go out and pollinate the entire farm.

The girls referred to some scenes from the *Bee Movie* and were impressed with my bee knowledge. We walked by the bee sanctuary, where I began my bee lessons with Henry. There was a sign on a stand near the door that read:

▌ Stewart Wedding Reception 4 p.m. to 9 p.m.

Henry was incredibly entrepreneurial. He optimized every aspect of the farm for beautiful events (and learning opportunities). We continued our walk past the garden that houses Henry's bench with the inscription to Catherine. We did not go inside, but the girls were curious; I told them it is a special place, and we should let it be.

Further down the path in yet another unexplored part of the farm was the smell of mint. We were curious about this and followed our senses to the H. Ives Family Farm herb garden. It was fenced in with a gate, and the different herbs had little identification cards. We spent a bit of time walking around, smelling each herb and trying to guess what our senses were telling us.

We correctly guessed lavender, basil, sage, oregano, mint, dill, but we missed cilantro and rosemary.

I could not help myself as I opened my phone and looked at the best herbs for pollination. I should have known! They all made the top 10 list of best herbs for pollination.

Our family headed back to the cabin before our chicken-coop activity.

I opened the Essentially Proximal emails and poured myself an early afternoon coffee. I felt energized to dive in. My husband was also firing away at his laptop, catching up on his emails. The close of Q2 fiscal second quarter was around the corner, and his team was preparing the forecast for Q3.

When we arrived at the coop, I had a thought that I wanted to find that darn rooster and...well, in the spirit of practicing my emotional intelligence, I will reserve what I was thinking. The calming energy from the herb garden this morning encouraged me to be more relaxed and focus on the moment. It occurred to me that every moment was kind of like my experience when I was taking pictures of the bees with the zoom on my camera. Whatever I'm looking at in life, I always get to choose my lens.

Speaking of energy, there were a lot of kids here today with chaperones. It looked like there may have been some sort of field trip.

The farmer helping us was amazing. He explained, "The chickens on this farm produce organic eggs, which means we only feed them organic grain. But these chickens love to eat other food, too. We have some special food that is their favorite."

He opened his hand to show a palmful of yellowish food.

"This here is bee pollen. Our beekeeper brings us the bee pollen from the hives, and they just cannot wait to eat it. Our chickens think this is the greatest treat – as you can see from their energy here.

"OK kids, and adults, go ahead to that bucket of organic grain and grab a handful! Start walking and spreading the food around."

The chickens were free range, so they all came out of the bushes and from every direction and started eating. There was another bucket of what appeared to be bee pollen. I asked the farmer if I could feed them that, and he nodded. I grabbed a handful of bee pollen and spread it around the coop. I took a peek inside the coop and noticed a lone chicken sitting inside.

I asked the farmer, "Why is that chicken not eating?"

The farmer put up his finger as if to say, hold on.

He told everyone to come over to the coop because we were going to start gathering eggs.

The coop was large. You could fit about 10 people inside, but there was a door that had a conveyor belt that led inside. The kids were all handed a basket and the farmer told them to start filling their basket with the eggs that would come out of the door. He hit a button and the automation began. The kids gently placed the eggs in the basket.

The farmer apologized for his delay in answering why that hen was not moving.

He said that sometimes one will decide to become a broody hen and will sit on her eggs until they hatch.

"What decides who becomes a broody hen?" I asked.

He said "There are some factors out of our control, like genetics, hormones, and instincts, but the lighting has something to do with it, too. When the days are long and the sun is shining, sometimes hens don't want to produce new eggs. They just want to incubate the ones they have."

These broody hens use their energy to make the eggs that produce babies. They do this by keeping the eggs warm and protecting the eggs until they hatch.

When you give time and energy to something, it encourages growth. When you have responsibility for nurturing others, you are responsible for making sure the environment you create is well suited.

Those new chicks were going to bring new energy to the flock.

"That broody chicken is a force of energy. What she puts her energy into will grow. And **what people put their energy into grows,** too." The farmer said it is important to be mindful of your energy – we need to create a warm environment to encourage life, which, in turn, will bring in new energy to the environment.

I nodded and recognized the message he was trying to convey.

The girls came running over with a basket full of eggs. The farmer excitedly said, "Well, girls, it looks like tomorrow's breakfast is all ready!"

We walked back to the cabin. The girls looked at their smartwatches and realized they had over 20,000 steps. This was a record for our vacation.

We made some dinner in the cabin (not chicken), and all got ready for bed.

The vacation was coming to an end, but the experience for us so far had been amazing.

I opened my email and sent a message to the leadership team. It read:

Dear Leadership Team,

When you give time and energy to something, it encourages growth. When you have responsibility for nurturing others, you are responsible for making sure the environment you create is well suited. Remember, what people put their energy into grows...

—Catherine

CHAPTER 13

Be Growth-Minded

I had never slept with noise-canceling headphones before, but Tom has shared his with me last night. This was the first day of our vacation that I slept past 8 a.m., and it felt great. There is something to be said for a good night's sleep and the impact it has on the mind and body.

When I woke up, I poured myself a cup of tea and went to sit on the porch of the cabin and enjoyed the zen. I looked around and took in the smells of the farm. I could see some families on their tractors making their way to the swimming hole and their various activities.

I wondered where my family might have gone, but it was kind of nice to sit in solitude and recharge. I thought about Henry and what he was up to today.

I recalled that we would be going on a ride today to see some of the many vegetables on the farm. I was thinking this was going to be on the less exciting side of the trip, but the kids had created the list, and we were all on board.

I debated whether to get up off this nice rocking chair and get some exercise, but I was so relaxed. One of the free-range chickens was making its way around my cabin, and it made me reflect on energy again: How we invest our time and energy is so important to growth. Henry had been giving me this sort of energy all vacation, whether he knew it or not. Perhaps I should ensure that he knew it!

I went inside, texted my family, and told them I was going for a walk. My husband told me to take my time; he was relaxing and reading a book, and the kids were swimming.

It was a beautiful day, not too hot, and the breeze was tossing loose leaves across the path. I walked toward the proximal part of the farm. I felt this was my spot. I was hoping to see Henry and catch up with him. As I approached the venue that had all the hives in it, I saw a young lady, maybe in her mid to late twenties, and she looked upset. I stopped and asked her if everything was OK.

She said, "I'm fine," but clearly she had been crying.

I tried to make her feel comfortable and asked if she needed to chat.

She said that last night at this wedding, she was the only one who did not have a significant other. She felt lonely and was longing for companionship in her life.

I introduced myself and asked her if she wanted to go for a walk. She said, "I'm Grayce, sounds good."

I led her over to the large metal sundial, and told her we were standing in the proximal – center – part of the farm.

I pointed out the grazing sheep and told her that it's OK to be vulnerable and bare like them. I showed her the beehives in the distance and explained how they're responsible for all this beauty on the farm. They are the source of growth for all the plants and flowers, and they nourish everything on the farm.

Grayce looked at me and smiled.

We continued our walk and came to the garden with the bench. I entered the garden with her, and we sat on the bench. I told her that we often look at the environment around us and compare. The wedding she went to drew up some emotions and feelings, which is OK, but that does not mean there is not a plan for you.

We stood up from the bench. I pointed to the engraving on the bench, which read:

"To my Catherine. I will patiently await the time we can see each other again. Please be patient and wait for me. I will tend to our hive. You are my queen bee."
Henry

Like me, Grayce delighted in the beauty of this message. She said she was starting to feel better.

She commented, "Life can be so messy, though."

I nodded and shared with her "**When life is messy, we have choices.** We can wallow in the mess and feel sorry for ourselves. Or we could try to unpack what caused our messiness and be agile to respond differently next time. Or we could pivot altogether and start anew. The choice is yours."

She asked me if I knew what was further down the path.

I responded, "I appreciate your curiosity – what a wonderful trait!" and we walked toward the garden.

She sniffed the lavender and commented on the aroma. "It is lovely," she said.

I told her that it was my favorite, too.

I told her that the bees love these herbs and use them to pollinate the farm. They are attracted to the scents. It pulls them in.

She thanked me for the chat, as we began walking back. We exchanged numbers and talked about our lives a bit. When we arrived back at the sundial, we saw Henry.

He was dressed in his beekeeper attire. It still looked like we had entered a biohazard area, but now I knew better! I introduced Grayce to Henry, and he said hello.

Grayce asked, "Are you the Henry from the bench in the garden?"

His voice became a little melancholy. "Yes, Grayce. I had that bench made for my wife, Catherine, when she passed away."

"Oh, what happened?" Grayce asked, like a child ready for a good story. I gave an embarrassed shrug at her lack of self-awareness, but Henry took off his mesh hat and moved toward a table overlooking the pasture. He knew I was curious about his wife and decided that this would be a good time.

We sat down at the table, and Henry leaned in as he told us their story.

"My wife and I opened this farm back in 1987 with 2,000 acres of land." We placed our first beehives right here on this spot. This is the proximal part – or the heart – of the farm. From there, we watched the farm take shape. We added more hives, flowers, vegetables, and gardens. We watched as the bees changed the landscape of the farm.

Henry said that people would come by and pick our fruits and vegetables. They started adding animals so their children could learn how to help feed and take care of them. They wanted the kids to experience the growth of our farm with us.

"Catherine loved the hives; she loved the bees and their contributions to growth," Henry said. **She knew that at the core of learning and growth was the bee and, as one of the beekeepers, she was responsible for spreading this growth to others.**

Catherine had passed away from a heart condition, Henry explained, but she wanted to build this sanctuary and host events here so people could experience what she experienced every day. She made me promise that I would keep the farm open to the public and find more beekeepers.

I could see Grayce thinking about this comment.

She asked Henry, "Is Catherine a beekeeper?" and looked directly at me.

Henry looked at me and smiled. "Well, I believe she just might be."

I looked at him skeptically. Did my conversation with Grayce make me a beekeeper? Had he overheard us talking?

We thanked Henry for sharing and we parted ways. For the remainder of the day, I wondered what he meant.

As my family and I walked through the crops, we had a chance to taste some of the fruits and vegetables. This was more like a farmers' market than a farm. They had jams made from fruits, vegetable dip, and other accoutrements. I picked up a jar labeled Catherine's Honeysuckle Essential Oil. I read the back: Nothing but natural ingredients. I smelled deeply, and it reminded me of the honeysuckle trees on the farm. It was lovely.

I asked the person selling where it was made, and she said right here on the farm. She said it was one of a kind – sold only here. I bought a jar to take with me. I could not wait to diffuse it.

Part of this vegetable-picking activity was that the kids got to fill a bag with whatever fruits and vegetables they wanted for dinner. The farmer labeled the bag so the chef could prepare the veggies the children picked to their liking. It was a nice touch. Basically, the kids got corn and carrots. Nothing green.

The farmer packing our bags said, "These crops here were all fertilized by our forager bees. They pollinated the crops, and the beautiful results you see here are going to be cooked by our chefs on the farm. Without our bees and, more importantly, our amazing beekeepers, these crops cannot grow into the most delicious and amazing tasting vegetables."

"What do the beekeepers do?" asked Gabby.

The farmer responded, "Once summer is underway, the beekeeper must maintain his hives and remove all the output and honey as it becomes ready for consumption. Bees must have an adequate hive, so they can thrive. As honey production accelerates, the beekeeper needs to add honeycombs to the hive so bees can deposit their honey. **The beekeeper is responsible for all the bees, their growth, and their ability to do the jobs that they were placed here to do.** If not for the beekeeper, nothing can grow!"

"Oh! It sounds like a fun job!" Gabby said.

As the farmer took our vegetables to the chef, the hostess escorted us to a table under a tent. This is where most of the dinners were housed each night. Tonight, the scene was lively. A band was playing music, kids were dancing, and families were eating, talking, and laughing. It was a jovial night filled with warmth and energy.

Just then, Grayce walked by with some friends. She introduced me to her group, and I introduced my family. She told her friends about the time we spent together in the morning and how I was a beekeeper. My family laughed and I chuckled.

"I am not an actual beekeeper," I said.

Grayce responded, "Henry thinks you are."

"What was that about?" Tom asked when they left.

"Honestly, I am not sure," I said. Henry called me a beekeeper today in front of Grayce.

"Interesting," he responded, "Well, maybe I will buy you a cute bee outfit when we get back." He gave me a flirtatious grin, and I winked back and smiled.

The kids came over and pulled us onto the dance floor, and we all danced and had a great time!

Later, after we went back to our cabin, I checked my emails. Nothing out of the ordinary. I sent an email that said:

Dear Leadership Team,

The beekeeper is responsible for all the bees, their growth, and their ability to do the jobs that they were placed here to do.

—Catherine

I smiled and went to bed. I was looking forward to the rooster and speaking with Henry in the morning about his beekeeping comment. Later my family would be taking a ride through the many fields of flowers to appreciate nature's beauty. It would be a perfect close to our vacation.

CHAPTER 14

Be Appreciative

I laid awake before the rooster crowed on Sunday morning, thinking about what I was going to say to Henry. I wanted to know what he had meant when he said I was a beekeeper. I reminded myself to continue my quest to Be Curious.

I took a jog over to the sanctuary, and no one was around. Henry was nowhere in sight. I didn't stay long. I kept my heart rate up and kept jogging. I ran past the garden and the herb farm. I followed the path further and came to a bridge that crossed one of those streams that likely connected the swimming hole and the lake where we fished. I continued to run. I went past the dairy farm, where I learned how to Be Nourished, I passed the pig pen where I learned that it's OK to Be Messy.

I kept jogging. I was on my second mile. I passed the chicken coop and thought how I can Be Energizing to others. I ran by some impatiens and quickly came to the fishing pond and continued to run along the bank. I saw the proximal part of the pond and the lilies from a distance. I realized how important it is to Be Patient.

The path looped around the swimming hole. It was still early. I kept running. I wanted to find Henry. I ran back to the large metal sundial. The sheep were all grazing in the pasture, and they seemed content in their bare vulnerability. My watch hit three miles. I was out of breath. I stopped and stood in the center of the sundial. I put my hands up over my head and took deep breaths as I walked to the fence. I leaned over the fence.

Just then I felt a sharp pain in my arm.

"Ouch!" I shouted. I looked at my arm that rested on the fence and saw a bright red welt.

I was just stung by one of those honeybees! It throbbed painfully. Thankfully, this was not the first time I had been stung, so I knew I was not allergic.

Just then, Henry emerged from the sanctuary. He took one look at the red mark on my arm and said, "That explains the hollering. Well, I think I have just the thing for you." Henry went back to the sanctuary and returned with a jar. "You mind if I put some of this on the sting?"

I was delighted to see him. "What is it?" I asked

"Well, it is Catherine's Caring Nectar. It is used to relieve pain. It has the essential oil of lavender and lemongrass, and it will help take the sting away."

He put a little on my arm, and it immediately felt better. He handed me the bottle and said I could keep it in case anyone got stung on our ride through the flowers later today.

"You know. That bee will not make it, Catherine."

"What do you mean?"

"It will die."

"I thought that was an old wives' tale."

"Some bees survive after they sting, but honeybees don't make it," said Henry.

"Why is that?" I asked.

"It is unique," he said. Henry explained that when a human gets stung, the skin of a person is so tough that the stinger gets stuck inside the flesh. The bee cannot fly away unless its stinger is amputated. So, it amputates itself and flies away, pulling the stinger out from its abdomen, which causes the bee serious trauma. It flies away, but it does not survive.

"That is so sad," I said.

"It's part of nature," said Henry. "But there is an important lesson to be learned here."

"Humans have tough skin, and they can take a lot of stinging, but it is the deliverer of those stings that often doesn't make it." Henry wiped the ointment off his fingers.

He said that regret sometimes leads to hurtful words that cause conflict, and this often has bad consequences. I understood. **Being appreciative of a human's tough outer layer is important, but we must be mindful of how those who aim to hurt or cause pain can be perceived. Lack of awareness here is often an inhibitor of collaboration and growth.**

It made sense, but I had never thought of it that way.

My arm was feeling remarkably better.

"Henry, why didn't you tell me you were in the essential oil business, too?" I asked.

"We're not, really. We make very little of this stuff, as we don't have the capacity to do this and run the farm. This is something we do on the side. We just enjoy using all the farms resources to help provide for each other."

I understood.

He asked how I was feeling, and I said fine.

I told him it was our last full day and I have come to appreciate this farm. I asked him why he called me a beekeeper the day before.

He looked at me with a smile. "What do you think beekeepers do?" he asked.

I thought hard about everything I had learned, and said, "The beekeepers ensure that their hive can thrive, and they capture all the output of the hive, such as honey, so the hive can continue to grow." I said that the environment around the hive had to have the proper conditions to ensure its growth. If you invest time and energy into ensuring the hive is thriving, the bees can provide rich reciprocity. They support the growth of our food supply, flowers, and much of nature's beauty all around us. It sounded simple, but I had learned a key truth at the farm: "The bees are at the core of growth," I said.

"Now tell me that is not spoken like a true beekeeper," Henry said.

"But I don't have any bees," I laughed.

"You most certainly do, Catherine. In both your personal and work life, you are one of the beekeepers that can help your hive thrive. You can develop new beekeepers. It's up to you to spread the pollen around so everything you touch turns into something beautiful."

Henry said, "You have to be appreciative for every opportunity you get to learn and grow. You are standing in this circle at the center of the farm, which is at the core of learning at growth. Whether you believe it or not, the lessons I have witnessed you learning and applying are those of a beekeeper."

I wondered again how much he had heard of my conversation with Grayce. Either way, I was appreciative.

I thanked Henry and told him I would stay in touch. I knew it might be the last time we saw him on the farm before we left.

We all hopped onto the flatbed truck lined with hay bales which was filled with enough hay on the floor to comfortably sit, too. It was the weekend, so we had a full truck. It was reminiscent of a hayride in the fall. The girls were delighted to see Helen sitting in the flatbed with us.

"OK, folks, it's time to Be Appreciative because you are about to witness some of the most beautiful flowers around," Helen said.

We traveled through fields and fields of flowers, each more colorful than the next. It was an amazing site. When we all got off, Helen handed all the ladies a sunflower.

"A bee!" Lilly exclaimed and dropped her flower.

I quickly picked it up and peered into the center. There most certainly was one feeding on the proximal part of the flower – gathering its nectar and getting ready to contribute to the growth of this beautiful farm.

I handed Lilly the flower and told her it would be OK. Just then the bee flew away.

"Off to pollinate," she said.

I told Lilly that that bee traveled up to three miles to find that flower, and would now go make honey and feed the colony so it could thrive.

We went back to the cabin, packed up our bags, and played one last board game.

I could not sleep that night. My mind was racing. It was going to be Monday when we got home, and I had so many thoughts running through my head. I decided to leave my team one last quote from the farm before I returned to work.

Dear Leadership Team,

Humans have tough skin, and they can take a lot of stinging, but it is the deliverer of those stings that often loses in the end. Regret and hurtful words that cause conflict often have consequences with bad outcomes. Being appreciative of people's tough outer layer is important, but we must be mindful of how those who aim to hurt or cause pain can be perceived. Lack of awareness here is often an inhibitor of collaboration and growth.

—Catherine

CHAPTER 15

Be

Proximal

On Monday morning, we packed the car to leave the farm. Everyone gave us a fond farewell. We said goodbye to Helen, and Henry made an appearance at the front drive. He handed me the recipes for Catherine's Caring Nectar and Catherine's Honeysuckle Essential Oil, along with a legal document granting us the exclusive rights to make and sell them through Essentially Proximal. There was one condition. We must come back and visit the farm each year.

I felt a tear trickle down my cheek and thanked him for that wonderful gift. I said I would certainly take him up on that.

On the drive home, the kids could not stop talking about the experience and how much fun we had on the farm. We cheerfully talked about everything we learned the whole way back. My mind drifted to Henry and the many lens-check moments he encouraged; who knew that a beekeeper could have such a profound impact on me and at a farm, nonetheless.

Tuesday came quickly and we were back to our routine. A rooster woke us up, but only because my kids had changed my phone alarm to be a rooster sound. We all had a good laugh that morning at breakfast.

After we got the kids to school, Tom and I headed to the office.

When we opened the door, we could not believe what we saw. Large posters with quotes were hanging along the walls.

They were all about bees.

We started reading the quotes as I walked the hallway to our offices.

They were beautiful.

We walked past the first leader's office, and he had a quote on the door that I had emailed. It said, "Be Curious."

As I continued down the hall, the quotes I had sent to the leadership team were posted on all of their doors. My husband and I looked at each other in awe.

We moved toward the factory and distribution center, and there was a beehive image on the door. It said:

Welcome to the Essentially Proximal Hive.

I was struck by a sudden realization. H. Ives Family Farms. It was HIVES Family Farm. How had I not made the connection before? Thinking back on my vacation experience reminded me of the power of what we choose to see.

We walked into the factory, and although it was early, the leadership team was already meeting. We walked over and said hello to the team. We sat down and talked for a while.

The team thanked me for the quotes and said that it was helpful and gave them new perspective on how we could work together. They said that over the last week, there were several *ah-ha!* moments.

They asked about the family vacation, and we talked about the farm, the activities, and how the kids enjoyed themselves.

I asked about what the Essentially Proximal Hive was, and one of the leaders, Beatrice, chimed in, "When we started getting your quotes, we realized that we are one big HIVE at Essentially Proximal."

Beatrice shared that the team had realized that it was us, as leaders, who were the queen bees, and we were responsible for helping our worker bees learn and develop. It was our responsibility to help pollinate or grow others and the company. The team realized something else, too.

"**To attract and retain our talent, we needed to create an environment that allowed people to thrive. At the heart of what we do is to 'cultivate a soul-nourishing experience through nature's beauty' – that is our mission,**" Amelia said.

As others in the room nodded in agreement, Amelia was encouraged to continue. She said, "When you shared your quotes with us from your holistic experience with nature's beauty, we all felt like we wanted to share them with others, too. When people come to Essentially Proximal now, they will see these quotes on the wall. They will know that we are a hive who works together and relies on each other to be successful – together."

Scott added, "At the heart of this company, we can use the Be mindsets that you sent us to encourage all of us to Be Proximal here."

If you keep your bees nourished, we can help fuel the growth of essentially proximal.

So, Amelia exclaimed, "You're our Be Keeper!"

Together, the team said, we can keep these Be mindsets alive, and we will recruit top worker bees and help this company grow.

I broke down and cried. I realized the transformation that had occurred. Ironically, the team identified that I had become a Be Keeper. Not so ironically, I thought back to my conversation with Henry about what it means to be a beekeeper. Like Henry does at the farm, I would ensure our hive thrives.

Later that week, we located the center of the Essentially Proximal building and put a large bee-striped circle with a diameter of three feet on the factory floor, with the words "Be Proximal." It symbolized the three-mile distance forager bees travel. It was a place for people to be together at the heart of our work.

As I consider our hive, I could not be more grateful for the family trip to the farm. Without realizing it at the time, I was at the core of learning and growth.

In one week, my lens had changed. Henry helped me see that small, incremental changes make a difference that can be lasting. I had transformed. I had become a Be Keeper. But this wasn't just about me, this was about us. We own what we see and how we decide to be. This is at the heart of what we do.

Before the close of the week, I sent a final quote:

Dear Leadership Team,

To attract and retain our talent, we need to create an environment that allows people to thrive. At the heart of what we do is to "cultivate a soul-nourishing experience through nature's beauty." That is our mission.

—The Be Keeper

Later that year, we launched our Bee Line of Essential Oils. Some of the bestsellers were Catherine's lines, produced directly from the recipe Henry had given us. We donated 50 percent of the proceeds from Catherine's lines to the H. Ives Family Farm. We visited the farm each year for the next five years.

Essentially Proximal became known for our nourishing culture and was recognized as a top place to work. We were attracting the best talent, people felt connected again, and that translated to both our internal and external customers. My leadership team embraced the Be mindsets, and I could see their professional and personal growth take shape as they pollinated others.

I had built a hive and developed Be Keepers to support it!

CHAPTER 16

*Be*coming a *Be* Keeper

Social media is remarkable. Only three years after visiting the farm and transforming the culture at Essentially Proximal, word was spreading of our culture. When individuals joined our company, they saw our personalized Be mindsets around the office. They posted these on LinkedIn and across other social media platforms. I would get direct messages from people asking if they could join our hive and work remotely. I was so encouraged.

People knew that the Be mindsets were our guiding principles, and we enacted what we espoused. Individuals were exhibiting significant personal growth. Leadership teams were crafting their leadership philosophies based on the Be mindsets. They were aligning these with their personal values.

We opened every meeting and townhall with a Be mindset. We talked about the hive, we remained open to those who had differing views, and we used those to challenge the status quo. Employees realized that by being open to our vulnerabilities we created a catalyst for growth and development.

I was actually asked to do a local TED Talk event, as word had gotten out on how our Be mindsets were transforming our culture. The TED Talk went viral. I started getting calls from other local businesses to help them implement Be mindsets in their organizations.

I did not know what was happening. I walked over and stood on our Be Proximal circle. My husband must have noticed; he walked into the circle with me. He hugged me and said, "Do you know where we are?"

I nodded, "We are at the Be Proximal circle and at the core of learning and growth," I said.

"Yes, we are," he said. "And you, you are the Be Keeper."

"You have transformed the culture at Essentially Proximal. These calls are no accident. You have earned the respect of your employees and leadership, not to mention others in the community. Your viral TED Talk is empowering leaders to transform their culture."

Tom said, "Maybe it is time to step away from being queen bee of this hive for a bit. It sounds like there are a lot of hives that need you. You have built a strong hive and you can appoint a new queen – a leader in this company that can transform themselves and others into Be Keepers."

"Why don't you go out and pollinate?" Tom said. "Develop other organizations to become Be Keepers. Help them learn how to be proximal."

I hugged him. I walked outside. I needed to call Henry. He has become my official mentor. He picked up the phone. I told him what had been happening. I wanted his advice. He asked if my hive was healthy. I said yes. He asked if I had developed Be Keepers at Essentially Proximal that could continue to support the growth of the hive. I said yes.

Henry laughed and said, "Well then, what are you waiting for, Be Keeper? Go forth and pollinate the environment around you!"

I launched my consulting company on May 20 – the same day that Henry's father had purchased the farm. It also happened to be my birthday, and, more recently, World Bee Day! World Bee Day was first observed on May 20, 2018, worldwide, to honor and protect the garden of pollinators.

A Leadership
Guide to Creating
a Thriving Hive

Are you curious about what was happening at Essentially Proximal while Catherine and her family were on vacation? Were you caught up in the emotion with Catherine as she saw her company culture transformed? Imagine being a bee on the wall at Essentially Proximal and watching firsthand the transformation take place over the course of Catherine's family vacation.

Well, you're in luck – there was a bee on the wall, and it wants to give you, the readers, a "peek inside the hive." If you want to learn more about how the Essentially Proximal leaders took steps to transform the culture after reading Catherine's quotes, then enjoy A Leadership Guide to Creating a Thriving Hive. Let's go *bee*-hind the scenes...

We hope you enjoyed reading *The Beekeeper*. As a reader, you probably caught onto the symbolism between the Beekeeper and transforming a culture and becoming a Be Keeper. This was done with intent. This part of the book takes you *bee*-hind-the-curtain at Essentially Proximal and provides insight into how Catherine's shared learning and inspiration from her farm experience were able to encourage her leadership team to act and transform the Essentially Proximal Hive. Appreciating how her emails were received by the leadership team and how they interpreted and personalized the Be mindsets served as a catalyst for transformation, which is the first step in applying them to your team or organization. The pollination and growth of others is an important responsibility. Although sometimes a difficult and challenging task, it has rich returns on shaping organizational culture.

Off to Vacation

Following a difficult townhall meeting, Catherine and her husband, Tom, said goodbye to the leadership team and headed out the front entrance of Essentially Proximal. They embraced in mutual support, recognizing that the meeting had illuminated some underlying culture issues. As they hugged, Catherine noticed the potted plants that adorned each side of the entrance to the building. The flowers were in bloom, and they looked beautiful. As they walked to their car, Catherine saw one of the factory employees walk out the door and give a sporadic, awkward wave. Catherine waved back.

"I almost got stung by a bee!" the employee said.

Catherine quickly recognized the wave was a "swat" and smiled as she said, "We should probably move those flowers away from the door."

"I think the bee flew inside..." he said. "Hey, enjoy your vacation. See you when you get back."

"Thank you!" Tom and Catherine said in unison.

And off Catherine and Tom drove to begin their vacation.

The Bee on the Wall's Perspective

The leadership team stuck around after Catherine and Tom left the townhall and had some open and honest discussions.

"Well, that was interesting," said Amelia, one of the more tenured leaders in the company in charge of marketing.

"Agreed. Transformational conversations can mean a number of things," said Suzanne from operations.

"I think Catherine doesn't realize she is growing Essentially Proximal too fast. She is saying yes to everything and everyone, and we are segmenting the company with essential oil product expansions that require meeting the needs of a new customer base and require massive new efforts. We are not set up to support this type of growth," Amelia added.

"The operations side feels the same way, Amelia!" Layla exclaimed.

"Same in sales," said Scott. "Our sales team is getting further and further away from its core competency, and that is why we are losing talented people. We have gotten into markets that are not profitable, and the sales team is fighting off new competition. They want to achieve their sales goals but are not aligned as to how this is going to be achieved."

"It sounds like Catherine and Tom are being a little too focused on growth and not the people," said Jessica from finance. "The human element has been lost."

"Happy hour, anyone? We used to go every Friday!" said Beatrice, from legal.

"*No!*" permeated across the room.

"It used to be fun, but this week was a challenge," said Scott.

They all felt that the energy from the townhall had been draining. The leadership team all agreed that they were not looking forward to those tough conversations when Catherine returned.

Everyone got up and left, calling out "Enjoy the weekend!" and "See you Monday!"

The bee that flew in the building buzzed through the office and found honey in the breakroom. As all the employees left the building, the bee enjoyed its own happy hour on the lid of the honey jar.

Pollinating an Organizational Hive

Discovery #1: Beatrice's Be Mindset

"Did you see that email from Catherine?" Amelia asked Scott with a smirk, as she poured a cup of coffee from the breakroom.

"Yeah, she must have been drinking," said Scott. "What the heck did she mean by *the hive is at the core of learning and growth and bees provide nourishment?*"

"It probably means that the beehive she was looking at on vacation feeds the farm. All I know is that I am curious to learn more," Jessica chimed in, as she overheard the conversation and entered the breakroom.

"Learning and growth, though?" said Amelia. "Come on!"

The group exited the breakroom with their coffees and went into a conference room, where they met every Monday morning to discuss important topics for the week.

Beatrice from legal was standing at the front with Catherine's quote on a slide.

"Did you see this?" she asked enthusiastically as the entire team walked into the room.

Dear Leadership Team,

The hive is at the core of learning and growth, and bees provide the nourishment for all things to grow. Bees work together and are focused on the same mission.

—Catherine

"Yes, we were just commenting on Catherine potentially overindulging and feeling prophetic in the moment," said Amelia.

Beatrice took over the conversation. "I think this is amazing that she sent this to us. I think she was having a moment. If we deconstruct this quote, she is making an important analogy for us. We, as the leadership team, are the leaders of the hive she is referencing, and we are at the core of learning and growth of our people at Essentially

Proximal. We are the bees that should all be focused on the same mission."

There was a smattering of polite laughter, as the team tried to get in on the joke.

"I am serious," said Beatrice. "I am going to embrace this quote and hang it on my office door. As a leader, I want my people to understand that I am the source of growth for them, and I want them to be nourished by continuing to learn and grow and embody our mission. If we want our people to stay and love to work here, we must enact what we espouse to be important," Beatrice passionately said.

That morning, she printed the quote on a poster board and hung it on her wall next to her office.

The employees at Essentially Proximal, regardless of function, passed her office. Beatrice felt it was refreshing to see how they responded. Some waved, some gave a thumbs up, some took photos, but it was the impact that the quote had on the other leaders that made Beatrice most inspired.

Beatrice did not realize her conversation was such a source of inspiration for the other Essentially Proximal leaders, as Beatrice received an email from all but one of them that day with the same theme. It said something to the effect that members of their functional teams commented on her quote, and that it seemed to make an impact! Little did all the leaders know there would be more to come.

Beatrice did something important here. As a leader, when others were seeing things from a place of negativity, she chose her lens and found the opportunity to inspire a shared vision. If you want to begin to transform your culture, you can start by embracing a simple Be mindset.

Be Inspired: It was Beatrice's goal to help others to Be Inspired. Her emotional energy was infectious. She had been told this before, so she leveraged her strength. She knew others might not act on Catherine's email, but after the townhall and the sentiment around Essentially Proximal, she knew Catherine wanted things to change. If she could be inspiring enough to convince the other leaders to focus on more strategic initiatives, then it could have a big impact on the culture.

Discovery #2: Scott's Be Mindsets

Employees began to filter into the office the next day. Scott, the sales leader, who sits across the hall from Beatrice, noticed a couple of them taking a selfie with the quote from Monday on Beatrice's wall. The poster board was white, but the letters alternated in yellow and black. It had the bee kind of feel. Beatrice's enthusiasm yesterday seemed to be infecting the organization. The employees were laughing and having a good time. Scott opened his laptop and saw the email from Catherine. He read it once, then read it again.

> *Dear Leadership Team,*
>
> *The hive must Be Nourished to continue to thrive, and the new bees that join the hive environment must be ready to contribute to the hive's success.*
>
> *—Catherine*

He thought to himself, *be nourished*, and began to self-reflect. He recognized that he may have not been the source of nourishment for his sales team over the last couple years, or the people he has been hiring may have felt less nourished by his leadership style. He has always taken a directive approach and focused on performance results. As a sales leader, this was his job – to drive the revenue line and help the organization achieve goals. As he reflected, he realized he was always telling people how to be successful. How he did things in sales. How he thinks the job should be done. Was this nourishment for his people, or was it draining? How was he providing fuel for people to grow?

He ran down to the printer with the quote. He asked them to put the quote on a black poster board and use white letters. He asked to have an image of a beehive complement the text. He added a special request to have a door nameplate printed with the words *Sales Hive*.

Scott picked up both items before lunch and placed the poster on the wall next to his office and the nameplate on his office door. You see, employees referred to his office as the "sales bunker" because all the meetings in that room seemed to be like a battlefield. People were taking shots, war gaming, or being told what to do in a combative fashion – the oppositive of nourishing a hive.

A head popped into the office; it was one of Scott's salespeople.

"The Sales Hive, huh?" he said.

"Yep," said Scott. "Care to sit down in the hive for a minute?"

"Oh, I think I will pass. I am quite unprepared for a sales performance discussion this afternoon," he said smiling. He knew what typically happened in that office.

This salesperson had been with the company since the beginning of Essentially Proximal. He was a top performer, but was not as engaged lately, and was very vocal in the townhall regarding the company culture.

"What if we just talked about you," Scott said, "not about the sales number?"

The salesperson nodded and walked into the Sales Hive. He spent over an hour with Scott. The conversation was personal. It was about development. It was more inclusive, and Scott was soliciting the salesperson's perspective on the business. Scott was doing more listening to understand than listening to respond. As the conversation went on, other salespeople were seen passing by and making comments. Scott wondered if colleagues were feeling sympathy for the salesperson, knowing what typically went on in the office.

The office door opened, and Scott and the salesperson shook hands. They exchanged a mutual thank you.

The salesperson pointed to the quote on the wall and gazed at Scott. "I felt this you know. I felt nourished," and walked away. Scott was filled with emotion. He sent a quick email to his sales team.

Sales Team,

I just opened the "Sales Hive," formerly known to all as the "Sales Bunker"; come by if you want to chat and connect. Sales metrics conversations will not take precedence in the "Sales Hive." Rather, we will engage in conversations about you, how we can thrive as salespeople, and how we can continue to develop every day.

—Scott

Scott's inbox was soon inundated with emails and text messages. He received everything from thumbs-up emojis to calendar invitations to meet in the Sales Hive!

There are some important leadership lessons if you want to transform your company culture into a thriving hive. Scott self-reflected on how he was being the source of growth for his team. The self-reflection process is critical to changing a culture. Organizations need to look in the mirror and determine how they can be an agent for change. For Scott, he recognized that he needed to take on this role as a leader in the company. He leveraged two Be mindsets to start transforming the sales team.

Be Nourished: The quote that Scott put up from Catherine on how leaders need to nourish the hive had a couple of underpinnings for transforming a company culture. For Scott, he recognized he might not be the source of nourishment for his team. Scott realized he might need to take a different approach by focusing on the development of human beings to achieve success and reinvigorate the team. Scott made the connection that when his team believed he was the source of nourishment for them, then other employees, or bees as Catherine referred to, would feel nourished, too.

Be Present: As a sales leader, it is easy to take the approach of telling people how to do things. While modeling the way is an important leadership practice, there also needs to be a balance between empowering others to bring new ideas and thoughts to the table. These different points of view can contribute to high performance. It is well researched that diversity of thought and voice are essential elements to a winning team, so we must consciously create space for that.

Discovery #3: Layla's Be Mindset

Now people were seeing two quotes from Catherine as they walked down the hall at Essentially Proximal.

Layla sat in the office and stared at her computer screen; she is very process-oriented, analytical, conscientious, and often skeptical. She questions everything and is very reserved. Her people tell her she is very hard to read, but she uses these strengths to lead the operations team. She looks at the facts and processes to optimize performance and always struggled with vulnerability. So, naturally Catherine's note piqued her curiosity.

> **Dear Leadership Team,**
>
> **Be Vulnerable with your team. This will accelerate your personal growth. Like the forager bee, you'll also pollinate the environment around you, providing the fuel needed for others to grow.**
>
> **—Catherine**

Layla jumped on the quote and sent a message to the leadership team that she was going to post this on her office door today! She beat everyone to the punch.

She decided to take a different approach to printing the quote and grabbed a big poster board and wrote the quote out by hand in this amazing calligraphy. No one knew calligraphy was a passion of hers. People were stopping by her office and admiring the writing. Layla had a team meeting planned with her operations team to focus on some supply chain issues with one of their vendors, but she decided to use this meeting differently. The team all met in a conference room. They were anticipating another meeting to discuss the supply chain disruptions, which are often exhausting.

However, when Layla entered the room, she brought the poster and hung it up for the meeting. Her team all stared at it, and she opened with...

"Did anyone know I love calligraphy?" she said.

Heads shook, no.

Layla began to tell the story of how she took a calligraphy class in high school and college and wanted to write wedding invitations. She talked about her passion for design and art, totally opposite of what the team was used to seeing with flowcharts and processes. She made a point to talk about how she never told anyone about this because she wanted to be taken more seriously and thought the art interests would diminish her credibility as an analytical and process-oriented professional.

Her team listened intently.

She was demonstrating vulnerability.

"You see this quote?" she said. "Together, let's strive to share more openly with each other. There is a tendency to lose the human element in the work we do, and creating a safe environment that welcomes vulnerability is the key to ensuring this doesn't happen. I just shared something very personal, and I want each of you to feel comfortable sharing something with others. I did not realize my mindset might have prevented the growth of our team. I want to be a forager bee, and I want each of you to feel comfortable pollinating others."

The group clapped!

"I want to share in our next meeting," someone said.

"Absolutely!" said Layla.

From there, the team started talking about supply chain issues. It felt different. People were more positive; the energy in the room felt different.

Layla rehung the poster on her wall so all could see.

There are important leadership lessons to be learned from Layla's experience. She identified a behavior she was struggling with and took advantage of the opportunity to lean-in and learn. Catherine's message had a profound impact on her. For the culture to change long-term on her team and organizationally, leaders should embrace the following Be mindset.

Be Vulnerable: Organizations need to embrace vulnerability as part of their culture. How many leaders share their personal story or leadership philosophy with their teams? This is an important part of creating that environment where people feel comfortable sharing and being open. The Be Vulnerable mindset should be part of every leadership development curriculum, because in the absence of this mindset, the human element is lost, which drives how organizations shape culture.

Discovery #4: Jessica's Be Mindset

It was midweek, and Jessica from finance was in the office early, looking at the month-to-date numbers. Between the supply chain issues and the new competitive entrants into the marketplace taking market share, the sales team was struggling to drive sales based on the macroeconomic environment. She buried her face in her hands and took a deep breath. Sitting up, she said quietly, "OK, girl, let's get at it," and opened her emails. There was another email from Catherine to her and the leadership team! She read the quote and had to laugh. It was the universe talking. The timing could not be more perfect.

Dear Leadership Team,

There are a lot of times life gets messy and we need to find creative ways to cool off and continue to flourish.

—Catherine

Be Messy — that's when the best ideas come to life, she thought to herself. She fired off a message to her finance team and said there would be an all-hands meeting at one o'clock to discuss some important topics. She was a bit vague, with the intent to surprise. She printed the quote on a poster board that mirrored the other leaders and maintained the colors that gave it a bee-like feel. As her team filtered in the office that morning, she could tell they were reading the quote as they passed by.

When one o'clock came around, the finance team made their way into the conference room with their computers ready to crunch some numbers. Jessica walked in with nothing. She smiled and asked if anyone saw the quote on her office wall; they all nodded.

"Does anyone remember what it said?" she asked.

An employee spoke up and said, "There are a lot of times when life gets messy and we need to find creative ways to cool off and continue to flourish."

"Yes!" Jessica said. "We need to be messy right now. There are several macroeconomic pressures out there impacting our teams, and we need to find meaningful ways to grow the top line while spending less. We need to roll up our sleeves, innovate, and be creative. That is what this afternoon is about."

The next three hours were different. The team felt empowered to use their voice and be creative. They came up with some ways to reduce expenses that would still allow the team to drive the sales number and put together a communication plan to share the news.

The leadership lessons from Jessica are important, as you look to transform your organizational culture. She modeled the way by changing the environment of her meeting. While most of the team came in ready to crunch numbers and look at spreadsheets, she approached things differently and allowed herself and her team to flourish.

The following Be mindset can be used in your organization to create a space for meaningful innovation.

Be Messy is the willingness to let your guard down and do things differently than what might have been done in the past. People need grace in the process of exploring and making mistakes. Learning opportunities come from being messy and using failure to propel growth. Jessica allowed her team of very conscientious and detailed individuals to put the pencil down for a minute and think creatively. This was uncomfortable at first but brought back the human element. Many organizations become hyper-focused on job descriptions and role clarity; even if your core competency is crunching numbers, a culture only thrives when diversity of thought and voice contribute in meaningful ways.

Shaping the Hive

The quotes kept coming in from Catherine, and the leadership team eagerly hung her inspiration throughout the office walls. It was amazing to see the transformation occurring. People had a revived skip in their step. The Be mindsets verbiage encouraged a common language. Some of the Be mindsets were more intentionally incorporated into meetings, and some were heard casually around the office.

> Don't let something pull you down, causing you to get all tangled up.
> There are rich returns when you can Be Patient.

"We need to be patient and really assess the supply chain issues going on. We can jump to assumptions about our suppliers and be quick to make a hasty move. We need to seek to understand," a leader overheard when passing by an operations team member's office.

> Be Calm in times when the environment around you may be causing anxiety or stress. People can sense when something is off and may communicate those feelings to others, causing an unwanted ripple effect.

Beatrice was delighted that one of her team members referenced Be Calm when they were meeting regarding patent infringement. She recognized that receiving an inquiry about a bestselling product line could induce a lot of stress. The Be mindset was front and center.

Discovery #4: Amelia's Be Mindset

There was one reluctant individual on the leadership team who had not embraced this newfound excitement around the Be mindsets. Amelia, who ran marketing – an important function of the company – was maintaining the status quo. Over the last few days, she had been giggling at some of the posters around the office, but this was her normal behavior.

Amelia sat down at her computer and reread the last two emails that had come in from Catherine. She absorbed them and questioned whether she was embracing these behaviors. She knew she might not be encouraging growth and nurturing others.

Dear Leadership Team,

When you give time and energy to something, it encourages growth. When you have responsibility for nurturing others, you are responsible for making sure the environment you create is well suited. Remember, what people put their energy into grows...

—Catherine

Dear Leadership Team,

The beekeeper is responsible for all the bees, their growth, and their ability to do the jobs that they were placed here to do.

—*Catherine*

Amelia looked up at the wall art hanging behind her desk. It read, "Believe in yourself and you will persevere." She paused. She always believed she needed to have faith within herself to be successful, but after considering Catherine's messages, she began to feel she might be unconsciously limiting her team. Perhaps she needed to outwardly accept *others*, believe in others, empower others, and create an environment that encourages growth for others. She needed to take steps to build her hive and support a culture of growth, which she realized she may have been failing to do. The marketing team was not feeling the same energy from her that other leaders were beginning to demonstrate this week.

Amelia took the two quotes from Catherine and printed them on posters. The quotes resonated and made her rethink her current behaviors as a leader. She hung them on the walls next to her office. She also created a sign that said, **"Welcome to the Essentially Proximal Hive"** and hung it above the factory entrance where many of the marketing employees and workers had offices. She took down the wall art behind her desk that read "Believe in your yourself and you will persevere." While believing in yourself is important, as a leader, she wanted her team to realize she was giving her energy to each of them to believe in their big potential.

There are important leadership lessons that can come from Amelia's *ah-ha!* moments. While it is very important to have high levels of self-efficacy and belief in yourself, as a leader, you must be intentional about believing in others to support ongoing learning and growth.

Be Growth-Minded. Organizations that invest in leadership development teach leaders to use the strengths of others and bring out the best in others to build organizational culture. Often, we see leaders taking credit for the hard work and ideas of their employees to elevate themselves. While the leader may be able to have a seat at certain tables, they should embrace opportunities to elevate their team in those meetings, highlighting the work of the team as a means for promoting and pollinating others. Nurturing employees' strengths is an important aspect of organizational growth. More importantly, ensuring employees feel energy from their leaders promotes growth, which is an important part of the Be Growth-Minded mindset as a leader. Modeling the way to pollinate and grow human beings is foundational to organizational culture.

The Journey of a Be Keeper

Bees are one of the most important pollinators of the environment. And while the beekeeper is responsible for ensuring the beehive thrives and is productive, within organizations everyone needs to work toward becoming a Be Keeper, like Catherine did for Essentially Proximal. Some questions for consideration.

- Who is a Be Keeper in your current organization?
- Who has been a personal Be Keeper for you?
- How much organizational effort would it take to transform your organization into a thriving hive?

These are questions leaders can ask themselves to create the environment needed for sustainable growth and development of their people, their culture, and the overall environment around them.

Throughout this leadership guide, you may have noticed how some of the leaders at Essentially Proximal responded to the emails from Catherine. There were differences in how these messages were received, which is not uncommon in organizations today. Let's examine some of the differences and how each individual embraced becoming a personal Be Keeper for their team, ultimately informing the culture.

Beatrice, from legal, demonstrated high levels of enthusiasm and energy; she wanted to rally the team despite reluctance. Her commitment to modeling the way to Be Bold and Be Inspiring became infectious energy for others to do some personal reflection, too. Organizations need individuals who can bring this energy and be a catalyst for change.

Too, it is important we leverage these individuals in culture work; their infectious energy can create the right conditions for change. Beatrice showed how to Be Bold by putting up the first Be mindset quote. She knew that by taking action, there would be followers, and followers she found.

Scott, from sales, had a reflective moment regarding the sales team. He had a dominant style and pushed toward execution, always. He realized he needed to Be Inclusive and listen to others' voices and less of his voice. When organizations put individuals in leadership positions who have demonstrated personal success, they need to ensure those new leaders are getting input from others to innovate and come up with new ideas. This becomes a catalyst for a culture change.

In addition, you notice Scott changed others' perception of interactions with him. This simple step of making his office a place where people can Be Nourished is a direction that seemed to impact his employee. Conversations about performance or business may be better suited to other places. Leaders have an opportunity to create a safe space in the office where employees feel fueled. When they enter the hive, they will nourish and Be Nourished.

Layla, from operations, was typically not a very open person. Her personality was a bit more private, and she did not share openly about herself, but her approach to Be Vulnerable opened the lines of discovery with her team. You may remember that there were some important supply chain issues that needed to be discussed, but Layla decided to lead the meeting and offer a more vulnerable tone. Sharing her passion for art and encouraging others to share at the upcoming meetings created an environment that fosters trust. The subsequent discussions they had on supply chain felt different.

Jessica, from finance, was finding anxiety in continuing to fund the growth of Essentially Proximal because of the macroeconomic environment. Her messages to the team were about allowing themselves to Be Messy. While structure is important, allowing a safe space for people to share ideas without fear allows for innovation and growth. She impacted her team culture by changing the perception of how a typical finance meeting would go. She let them get messy, which sparked ideas to help achieve organizational goals.

Amelia, from marketing, was more skeptical and reluctant to embrace a culture change early. During the week, she saw others moving toward embracing the emails Catherine was sending, but she initially held back. Why do leaders sometimes not embrace new cultures? In a rapidly changing corporate world, organizations are faced with the difficult task of helping their employees find meaning. Each employee has different needs and gets energy differently. We may not fully know why Amelia was hesitant and what changed her mind, but the other leaders around her were a source of inspiration to help move her along.

As she sat and read the quotes from Catherine, which were about nurturing and inspiring others to do their best work, it seemed she was unconsciously limiting her efforts to nurture and inspire others. As a leader, she recognized that her success is dependent on the team she supports, and it is she who needs to provide the fuel to her team to learn, grow, and develop.

Pollinating Your World

As you learned, we are not limited in our Be mindsets; you can choose how to be. Anyone who thinks they're too small to make a difference has never met the honeybee. Catherine's decision to share her experience at the farm with her team helped her see that small, incremental changes make a difference that can be lasting – in this case, transformative. The members of the leadership team recognized the power of owning what they see and how they each decided to be. This became the heart of what they do, individually and even more, as a team. The most beautiful part about this transformation is that each person saw the opportunities through a different lens; they were able to authentically and unapologetically lean into the vulnerabilities of discovering new ways to see and subsequently be. So, tell me, Be Keeper, how will you pollinate your world!?

Connect with us at www.leadershipfables.com

Acknowledgments

My heart is smiling to author this important piece of our story. I am eternally grateful for this gift. It is the people in my life who are the heart of ongoing learning and growth. All my love and expressions of gratitude are extended to my mom, dad, and sister for giving me the roots to grow, to my husband and two daughters for giving me wings to fly, and to each additional member of my star system for inspiring the ebb and flow of our journey. We are certainly brighter, better, richer, and stronger, **together.**

Hugs & love, Katie xo

Thank you to the Beekeeper who inspired this story, my wife and daughters for their unconditional love and support, to my mom, dad, and sister, who always encouraged me to be myself and leverage my strengths, and to the people in my life who have been my personal source of growth and inspiration.

Love always, Michael G.

Author Bios

Katie P. Desiderio counts her blessings starting with the people in her life, which guides her approach to work where her focus is on every organization's most important asset – you! Her personality and behavioral attributes emphasize collaboration and all things that keep human beings in focus, which fuels her intrapreneurial spirit.

As an athlete, she found flow in sports and later discovered flow at work to fuel her professional trajectory.

After working for several years in corporate marketing, Katie chose a second career in higher education, where she celebrates the honor of being the first female chairperson of the Economics and Business Department at Moravian University, the sixth oldest institution in America and first to educate women.

As the mama of two extraordinary girls, she is committed to the development of rising leaders, namely in the spirit of leading from any seat. Along with her work as a tenured faculty member at Moravian University, Desiderio is Principal Partner in Learning of Proximal Development, LLC, an authorized DiSC partner, specializing in leadership development and the advancement of performance through learning.

Katie's personal mission is grounded in her r²C model, where she has devoted her work to *recognize* what we give our time and energy to grow, to *reflect* on how we [choose to] interact with and see the world, and, at the heart of her approach, to *connect* with why this fuels transformative growth. This model is delicately nurtured in the interplay of our mindset and our [mindful] behaviors, so when she falls along the way, she chooses to fall up. This inspires her to lead with *grace* while tickling curiosity and encouraging discovery in working with and through others.

Upon completion of her doctorate in Organizational Learning and Leadership, Katie has been co-authoring scholar-practitioner journal articles, conference proceedings, and now this book with her learning partner and friend.

Michael G. Frino was always told he was creative and had a vivid imagination during his childhood. He parlayed this feedback into a passion for writing and storytelling. He published his first poem in 1993 titled *The Human Tree* and is the author of *Welcome to Waycool School* (2010) and *Waycool School Takes the Bus* (2011) children's book series. In addition to writing, Michael has over 20 years of professional experience working for Fortune 500 companies in sales, leadership, and organizational development across the payroll/human resources, pharmaceutical, and med-tech industries.

Michael finds his flow state today from helping organizations transform their culture with a focus on the growth and development of human beings. His curiosity on how organizations optimize performance at work inspired him to obtain his PhD in Organizational Learning and Leadership in (2010) and embrace opportunities to help individuals, groups, and organizations reach their peak potential. His co-authoring of *The Beekeeper* is the culmination of decades of research and publishing with his friend, Katie P. Desiderio, in performance improvement journals to understand how organizations can provide transformational growth to their most important assets, people.

Join Katie and Michael on this journey to inspire how you can pollinate the world!

Index